Synkrētic

The Journal of Indo-Pacific
Philosophy, Literature & Cultures

2022 / № 3

Synkrētic
The Journal of Indo-Pacific Philosophy, Literature & Cultures

ISSN 2653-4029

Editor: Daryl Morini
Deputy Editor: Christian Romuss
Associate Editor: Devon Turner

www.synkretic.com

General enquiries: enquiries@synkretic.com

Correspondence should be addressed to

   The Editor, Synkrētic Journal
   c/o Irukandji Media Pty Ltd
   Unit 9 204 Alice St
   Brisbane City Qld 4000
   AUSTRALIA

Synkrētic acknowledges the traditional custodians of the lands of Brisbane on which we work, the Turrbal and Jagera peoples.

Published in Australia by Irukandji Press, Brisbane.

Irukandji Press is a trade name of Irukandji Media Pty Ltd.

ISBN 978-0-6454980-1-1

Layout and editorial matter: © Irukandji Media Pty Ltd, 2022

Essays, responses, stories and notes: © retained by respective authors or their estates and (re)printed here with permission OR source is in the public domain.

The moral rights of the authors have been asserted.

All rights reserved. No part of this publication may be reproduced, stored in a retrieval system, or transmitted in any form by any means without the prior permission in writing of the Editor of Synkrētic.

Cover design and typesetting: Arthur Arek

Contributors

Marceline Até · Amie Batalibasi · Dorell Ben
Ben Gaskin · Bronisław Malinowski
Leonardo N. Mercado · Daryl Morini
Claire Moyse-Faurie · Philibert Nékaré
Corneille Nonké · Marinette Oundo
Jioji Ravulo · Martyn Reynolds · Anouk Ride
Kabini Sanga · James D. Sellmann
Maria Thavivianon

Acknowledgments

Synkrētic №3 (Dec. 2022) was a collaborative enterprise involving 17 past and modern writers and oral history sources from 7 countries across the region.

Contributors to this issue were based in New Caledonia (6), Australia (5), New Zealand (2), the Philippines (1), Solomon Islands (1), the United Kingdom (1), and Guam (1).

Synkrētic warmly thanks all rights holders from around the world whose support made this issue possible, and especially the people and organisations listed below.

The Council for Research in Values and Philosophy
Routledge & Kegan Paul Ltd
Dr Claire Moyse-Faurie

Contents

The magic of Melanesia — 1

ESSAYS

Leonardo N. Mercado
On Melanesian philosophy — 5

Kabini Sanga & Martyn Reynolds
The pattern for a good life:
Indigenous Solomon Islands ethics — 23

RESPONSES *Pasifika thought in modern Australia*

Anouk Ride
An Australian in Honiara — 45

Jioji Ravulo
Listening to Pasifika voices — 52

Amie Batalibasi
The ripple effect of blackbirding — 59

James D. Sellmann
On Pacific logic — 64

STORIES

Dorell Ben
He — 73

Bronisław Malinowski
The jumping stones — 79

Claire Moyse-Faurie et al.
The first people — 83
    TRANSLATED BY *Daryl Morini*

NOTES

Ben Gaskin
Daya Krishna and Twentieth-Century Indian
Philosophy *by Daniel Raveh* (Review) — 91

EDITORIAL

The magic of Melanesia

In this third issue of *Synkrētic*, we navigate to Melanesian waters.

We begin in Papua New Guinea, where the Filipino missionary Leonardo N. Mercado lived in the late 1980s. His observations on Melanesian culture, philosophy, and on several languages spoken in the highlands remain relevant to the modern reader. Remembered as one of the leading Filipino philosophers, Fr. Mercado notes the similarities between his and Melanesian culture.

In the next piece, an excerpt from the celebrated anthropologist Bronisław Malinowski's influential *Argonauts of the Western Pacific* (1922), we join a fleet traversing the Trobriand Islands that lie scattered off the east coast of Papua New Guinea. His account captures one tribe's feat of navigation and the glorious magic of Melanesia, with the fleet vying to escape a giant octopus, homicidal rocks, and witches to survive the trip.

Further south, the magic continues in an excerpt from Dr Claire Moyse-Faurie's collection of Indigenous Kanak oral history from New Caledonia, newly translated for this journal, in which brave women are turned to stone for disobeying orders, a mountain walks and crows like a rooster, and an undead chicken calls from inside his killer's stomach.

Tacking northwest to reach Solomon Islands, the essay by Victoria University of Wellington's Associate Professor Kabini Sanga and Dr Martyn Reynolds on ethics provides rich insights into the ethical framework of the Gwailao clan of East Malaita. This thought-provoking piece challenges non-Indigenous researchers to question their 'Western-biased ethical system that assumes individual rights to be paramount' over local ethical systems that are 'exoticised' by the academy.

Staying in Solomon Islands, the filmmaker Amie Batalibasi discusses the impact of the painful and unresolved legacy of the blackbirding trade, the enslavement of 60,000 Pacific islanders on Queensland's sugar plantations, on her native Malaita and descendants in Australia. Offering a unique perspective, Dr Anouk Ride reflects on her experience as an Australian in the country's capital, Honiara, during the 2021 riots and COVID-19.

We sail southeast to the easternmost tip of Melanesia in Dorell Ben's charming short fiction "He", a story about a son's fraught homecoming on his native island of Rotuma and his new beginnings on the Fijian mainland. On a different island, the Fijian-Australian University of Sydney Professor Jioji Ravulo, the first Pasifika professor in Australia, shares his passion for supporting Pacific islanders through research, social work, and music.

Heading back north to Micronesian waters, the University of Guam's Professor James D. Sellmann observes that Pacific logic is non-correlational, meaning that something can be both true-and-false, unlike either-or logic baked into Western thought by Aristotle.

We finally reach the subcontinent, the end point of this issue's journey, with Ben Gaskin's review of Professor Daniel Raveh's *Daya Krishna and Twentieth-Century Indian Philosophy* (Bloomsbury Academic, 2020). This reflective piece strikes up a memorable conversation with the colourful and incisive Indian thinker who, in an earlier issue (Issue 1, 'The West's goddess of reason', 46-57), also blew on the cobwebs of Aristotelian logic like his Pacific friends.

Daryl Morini

ESSAYS

On Melanesian philosophy*

Leonardo N. Mercado†

Is there a Melanesian philosophy? Before the question can be answered, there is another question: Is there a Melanesian identity? The word Melanesia applies to Irian Jaya, Papua New Guinea, the Solomon Islands, Vanuatu, New Caledonia, and Fiji. Melanesia is different from Micronesia and Polynesia. In Papua New Guinea alone the three million inhabitants have over 750 languages[1] and even their physical features vary, such as skin pigment which ranges from light brown to charcoal black and hair from kinky to straight. Furthermore, the contacts of Melanesia with Western technology and ways have brought about culture change. Is there then a Melanesian identity? Bernard Narokobi's[2] series of newspaper articles entitled 'The Melanesian Way' caused a controversy.[3] Letters from readers affirmed his contention of the Melanesian Way, while others denied it.

As an example, all the members of a family look different, yet they may also have physical or moral features which are common.

---

* First published in Vol. 18 (1988) of the journal *Catalyst* by the Melanesian Institute for Pastoral & Socio-Economic Service, this essay appeared as 'Appendix C: Melanesian Philosophy' in Leonardo N. Mercado, *The Filipino Mind: Philippine Philosophical Studies II* (Washington, D.C.: Council for Research in Values and Philosophy, 1994). This lightly edited version is republished with the gracious permission of the Council.

† Fr. Leonardo Nieva Mercado, SVD (1935-2020) was a pioneer of Filipino philosophy. Ordained in 1964, he served as a missionary in Papua New Guinea from 1985-1988. He lived in Quezon City, the Philippines.

In short, they have a 'family resemblance' (an expression which Ludwig Wittgenstein popularised in philosophy). Although the Melanesian countries may vary in many ways, they have a family resemblance. Just as the countries of Europe vary from each other, there is such a thing as the so-called European way, European culture, or European thought. So, there is a Melanesian identity just as there is an African identity.

Melanesian identity may be compared to the uniqueness of Melanesian Pidgin. Although it has borrowed many words from English and German, it is not broken English. It has developed its Melanesian-flavoured speech patterns and syntax over a century.[4]

If there is a Melanesian identity, there is also a Melanesian philosophy. Philosophy is taken here not in the scholastic or existential meaning but in the anthropological sense such as Filipino philosophy.[5] Man has been the focus of modern philosophy. While human nature is partly universal, it also has particular aspects such as those affected by culture. If philosophy is to be anthropocentric, it must join the ranks of the social sciences, but if philosophy is a social science then its findings are approximate, unlike the findings of the rigorous physical sciences. Melanesian philosophy is then an approximate interpretation of the Melanesian mind.

Since there are various Melanesian cultures, can one speak of a Melanesian philosophy? Assuming the average Melanesian is five feet and seven inches tall, there are shorter and taller ones and they all may be illustrated in a bell-shaped curve. Likewise there are totally traditional Melanesians who may not have seen a white man at all while there are also Melanesians in cities who are over-exposed to Western ways. In spite of this variety, there are typical Melanesians and Melanesian philosophy is their worldview. How the typical Melanesian is attained will be explained in the following section on methodology.

I. The methodology

As mentioned earlier, Narokobi's articles (which eventually were compiled in book form) caused a controversy after publication. The main weakness of his work is its lack of strict methodology. As a

Synkrētic

poet-journalist-lawyer he uses a more intuitive approach in reaching his conclusions. The editor of the compiled volume suggests that the confusion caused by the controversy calls for 'a debate that requires a systematic, reflective and intellectual rigour.'[6] The methodology used in studying Filipino philosophy can also be employed in attaining Melanesian philosophy;[7] put briefly, this analyses language and behaviour. Since the methodology has been explained in the book mentioned above, there is no need to elaborate it again. Instead, we shall analyse Melanesian Pidgin because it reflects the thinking of the people who speak it. It is true that Pidgin is spoken less in the Papuan side and that there are variations of Melanesian Pidgin. While Pidgin has been developed as a business language, there has been some degree of creolisation by which it is spoken as a first language.

Together with Pidgin we shall analyse Melpa, a dominant language in the highlands of Papua New Guinea. In the process of language analysis, we noticed a strong correlation of the findings from both Pidgin and Melpa. A similar trend was found in two other local languages. We suspect the same will be true of the other Melanesian languages and recommend that research be made in that direction.

A phenomenology of Melanesian behaviour can reveal its corresponding philosophy. In other words, where a pattern of behaviour is established, an explanatory rationale can be deduced.

Almost all the examples to be cited come from Papua New Guinea, the findings would seem to apply also to the rest of Melanesia. The whole of philosophy may be grouped into three areas: man, world, and God. Here we shall look for a Melanesian philosophy of man, world, and God. This will be in sketch form as must every pioneering venture.

II. Philosophy of man

This section will discuss the Melanesian as individual, as thinker, and as social being.

On Melanesian philosophy

The Melanesian as individual

The word *bel* illustrates how language is a window of the mind. The usages are indicated in the tables. What do the tables reveal? Firstly, while there is no one-to-one ratio between Pidgin and Melpa, they have much in common. The tables show how Pidgin somehow reflects the thinking of Melanesian languages.

Secondly, there are gaps in the Melpa counterpart because Melpa uses other interchangeables. Thus in Table 10[8] *tingting long bel* is translated as *numan pili napila* (to reflect, think, meditate). Likewise in Table 11 *bel klin* may equally be translated as *kitim kai* or as *numan kai* (sincere). But *wanbel* is *numan tenta* (unity, agreement) and not *kitim tenta*. Likewise *tanim bel* is *numan robolro* (to be converted).

What can be gathered from the above? They indicate that the Melanesian does not compartmentalise his faculties, much unlike some people who separate their emotions from their thinking. The Melanesian thinks holistically. The same can be seen in the word *lewa* which is not only physiological (liver, heart, spleen, innards), but also intellectual (mind) and volitional (desire, seat of emotions).

The Melanesian as thinker

How the Melanesian thinks can be deduced again from his language and behaviour. Since Pidgin is a concrete language, abstract English words, for example, have to be translated in a roundabout way. If the language is concrete, how do people reason out? Their usual way is to use metaphors and allegories *tokbokis*.[9] For instance, 'you cannot catch two pigs at the same time' can have varied applications. A man who wanted to prove that having two wives is all right said, 'I do not steal if I dig sweet potatoes from my own garden.'

While the Westerner thinks in either/or terms, the Melanesian counterpart is both/and.[10] For example, a Westerner may judge things as either dead or alive, but for the Melanesian a particular rock may both be dead and alive.[11]

Elsewhere we have explained the two approaches to truth: deductive and inductive.[12] Deduction proceeds from abstract premises

Synkrētic

and arrives at concrete conclusions through cold logic; this approach suits the abstract Western mind. The other logical way is to proceed from the concrete and infer the abstract through intuition; the Melanesian thinks in this way.

The Melanesian as social being

The language reveals much of the social philosophy. Whereas the pronoun 'we' has only one form in English and other European languages, Pidgin has two forms: *yumi* (inclusive form) and *mipela* (exclusive form). Whereas the Western languages stress gender (such as he, she, it in English; *der, die, das* in German; the masculine, feminine and neuter nouns in romance languages), Pidgin has no concern for gender. He, she, and it are rendered as *em* (although *en* can only be for neuter). The language of greetings can also be revealing. Whereas a simple 'Good afternoon' in English will suffice, Pidgin will specify the addressee (that is, if they be two, three, or four): *apinun tupela/tripela/fopela*.

The social concern is also reflected in Melpa. 'Hello' in Melpa (which literally means 'you are coming') is *wuyo* for one person, *wilo* for two persons, and *wuyo* for three or more persons encountered on the way. Likewise, 'goodbye' (which literally again is 'you are going') is *piyo* for one person, *pilo* for two, and *puyo* for three or more persons.

Kinship terms also disclose the social thinking. *Papa* and *mama* can mean any elder of one's tribe and not necessarily one's biological parents. Every member of one's age level is called *brata* (brother) or *susa* (sister).

What do the foregoing linguistic data indicate? They show that the Melanesian is group-conscious and not individualistic. More of this can be seen in the *wantok* system. Since Melanesian society is evolving, let us trace the phenomenology of the *wantok* system from the traditional to the modern context. In traditional Melanesian society, one's identity was tied up with the tribe. This is so deeply rooted that even expatriates are asked about their tribal affiliation. The tribe is the source of one's protection and life in general. That explains why people give money for bride-price, contribute food for funerals, and offer their lives in tribal fights. Compensation for accidents also takes a tribal perspective. If one member is hurt, the whole tribe is involved. Melanesians support their aged parents, divorced sisters, *etc.*, as a matter of duty. We shall not dwell here upon leadership which is egalitarian, unlike the hierarchical or pyramidal style of the Polynesians.[13]

If the Melanesian leaves his place and goes to another surrounding, he will not forget his tribe-oriented behaviour and thinking, but will form or join another tribe known as *wantok* where he retains a similar network of social relationships.[14] 'In a limited sense, *wantoks* are people who have a common language, while in a broader sense, *wantoks* are people who understand and support each other.'[15] Thus, if a highlander goes to Port Moresby, all highlanders, including those from enemy tribes back home, become his *wantoks*. In urban areas, settlements are often based on geographic origins. That means that there are areas for coastal migrants, for highlanders, and for those from the islands.

When Melanesians go abroad they also form a *wantok* system, but based on a national system. If a stranger meets an accident in a town, all the people of his province in that town will help him. This behaviour would be impossible in the West. University students in Lae and in Port Moresby group themselves into regional alliances. The new 'tribe' functions in a manner similar to those in a traditional setting, that is, for protection, for revenge in case of harm sustained by any member, for seeking of compensation, *etc.* Whereas the Simbu and the Hagen students may be enemies back home, they form one 'tribe' with other highlanders on the university campus.

The core of Melanesian social philosophy is reciprocity as expressed in brotherhood and harmony.[16] This is seen, for instance, in the bride-price exchange among the highlanders or in the bride exchange among the lowlanders. This is also seen in the ending of hostilities where both warring tribes become friends again through the exchange of pigs and other valuables.

Synkrētic

An example of this exchange may be seen in the decision made by a village court which reflects traditional thinking. Two men broke into the house of a male catechist and stole his valuables. The catechist found the thieves and hurt them in a fight. The village court decided that the thieves pay 200 kina to the catechist for stealing. But the latter was to pay 140 kina for hurting the thieves.

Reciprocity has always been pragmatic. Even the big man who throws a party expects his guests to give him status. According to Narokobi, 'cooperation and mutual support, especially in times of need and crisis are part of our living experience. Confrontation and competition are kept to a minimum.'[17]

Is individualism absent in this social philosophy? In the traditional setting a child may disobey his parents, but when the community or the tribe is at stake, the child has to toe the line. A member will offer his life in the case of a tribal fight; this is unthinkable for the Westerner. We do not deny that some form of individualism is creeping in because of modernisation. For the typical Melanesian, however, the good of the group takes precedence over himself.

III. Philosophy of the world

In this section we shall discuss time, space, property, and law.

Time

"PNG time" has the derogatory meaning of being tardy by about one hour. But being unpunctual is symptomatic of a different philosophy of time, as can be gleaned from the language and behaviour.

Western languages usually have many tenses. The present tense in English, for example, has the simple present, present perfect, and present progressive. If the past, present, and the future tenses are multiplied with their three corresponding forms, the total is nine! But this "excess" of tenses is absent in Pidgin. According to Mihalic, 'verbs have no real tense forms in Melanesian Pidgin. Time relations outside of the present are expressed with the help of adverbial modifiers.'[18] Thus 'I am reading' may be translated as *mi stap rit* or *mi rit i stap* or *mi rit nau* or *mi wok long rit*.[19]

Nau is much broader than the English 'now' because the former can also mean 'today.' Suppose one asks, *em bai kam long wanem taim?* (What time will he come?), the answer from a Melanesian can be *nau tasol* (right now). The European who is used to his restricted meaning of now may have the frustration of waiting for hours or the whole day.

In the Simbu language the equivalent of 'yesterday' can mean 'tomorrow', but also can mean 'yesterday.' The Simbu language is more concerned about whether or not a particular action is finished than about tense.[20] The same is true among the Mogeis, a Melpa-speaking tribe of the Western Highlands.

Natives distinguish two kinds of verbal action, complete and incomplete. Both are indefinite, in the sense that in the verb form itself, the idea of time is not indicated, or the time element can be understood from the context itself.[21]

Thus *na punt* can variously mean 'I am going', 'I went', or 'I shall go'. Time has to be specified by other markers like *na agup punt* (I am going now).

The Melanesian speaks more of time in relation between himself and the world. A few examples: *taim bilong dai* (at the hour of death), *taim bilong draiwara* (at ebb tide, at low tide), *taim bilong kaikai* (mealtime), *taim bilong pait* (wartime). The Melanesian uses *taim* with the weather and the seasons such as *taim bilong ren* (rainy season), *taim bilong hangre* (season of hunger), *taim bilong san* (dry season), *taim nogut* (bad weather), *mit tambu taim* (lent), *etc. Taim* can also mean 'when', 'while', 'then.'

How the Melanesian behaves also reflects his time orientation. It is common knowledge that Melanesians in general do not know their age or their birthdays. Keeping historical records has not as yet generally occurred. But people in Kundiawa (Simbu Province) are reported to reckon events as *bifo long Jumbo o bihain long Jumbo* (before Jumbo or after Jumbo).[22] Jumbo was the first elephant they saw in 1973. This significant event was their point of time reference. When the sick woman in the Western Highlands was asked about the date of her last confession, she replied: 'That was when our communion minister was still alive.' Although some Melanesians may sport cheap quartz watches in rural areas, they may still be late because the wristwatches may serve more as decorations than as timepieces.

What then is the Melanesian philosophy of time? Time may be viewed either as cosmic or as human.[23] Cosmic time stresses time as linear, that is, as either past, present, or future. This is peculiar to Western languages with their emphasis on the tenses. Western languages may be linear or tense-oriented as an effect of the four seasons. The winter season forces people to store food in summer and autumn when it is plentiful. But this future concern is not needed in Melanesia where it is spring and summer throughout the year. They would resemble more the southern Europeans (such as lower Germany, lower Spain, or lower Italy) who differ temperamentally from their northern counterparts.

The Melanesian is more inclined to measure time with himself as the reference. In the examples given above, events are measured according to their relevance to the individual and to his group. Events still remembered belong to the 'living memory time' and those earlier belong to 'ancestral time' (*taim bilong ol tumbuna*).[24]

The latter stores the people's values and mores and is also the focus of myths and the superhuman. Time for the Melanesian is not an absolute because his community takes centre stage. What has meaning to him and to his community has relevance in time; what is outside man is in chaos. Time then, insofar as it has meaning to the Melanesian, is relational.

Linear time, which is oriented to the clock and the calendar must be adjusted to by those working in offices and factories, as well as children who attend school, because of the inroads of urbanisation. But the typical Melanesian will be more prone to human, than to linear, time.

Space

Space and time go together. If the Melanesian philosophy of time is different from the Western concept, so is its idea of space. Here language again is a window for looking at Melanesian thinking. The

On Melanesian philosophy

Pidgin word *long* is intriguing. European languages as exemplified in English have prepositions like of, in, on, at, to, from, with, about, because of, and during. All these words are rendered as *long* in Pidgin.[25] Furthermore, *long* is used with indirect objects, *e.g., givim kaikai long mi* (give me food). It is also used with adverbs and in adverbial phrases, *e.g., antap long* (on top of), *bihain long mi* (behind me), *klostu long mi* (near me). The above linguistic clue suggests that space is linear for the Western mind, but nonlinear for the Melanesian.

Space for the Melanesian is not abstract, but concrete and personal. For him land is demarcated by trees and rivers, not by some imaginary line crossing the land. He also thinks that not all space is equal because he believes that spirits occupy some places. On the other hand, space for the Westerner is abstract, a boundless extension and infinitely divisible. The equator, latitudes and longitudes are examples of imaginary lines dividing abstract space.

Like time, the Melanesian looks at space from his sense of meaning according to which space is significant insofar as it concerns his community or group. What stands outside human relevance is non-space.

Property

The philosophy of private property stems from its corresponding social philosophy. If the social philosophy enshrines the individual, this has its implications. 'The Western concept of private property can be traced back to the Roman juridical concept of absolute ownership whereby the owner has the absolute right to use, abuse or not to use his property without any obligation to society.'[26] But the Melanesian philosophy of being, centered on community, situates the individual in the context of his community so that property takes a communal dimension.

Traditionally, the great man shared his wealth with others. The more receivables he had, the more he was considered rich, although his house may not look different from that of his neighbours. If a person did not share his goods there were mechanisms (such as adverse comments and ostracism) to make him toe the line. But the advent of modernisation has protected selfishness. A famous New

Synkrētic

Guinea politician who died in office was discovered to have fortunes deposited in foreign banks.

The coming of Western culture also introduced the concept of private property. Melanesia has become a battleground between the concept of property as absolute and the concept of communal ownership where the owner is only a steward.[27] This conflict is better understood when placed in the context of legal philosophy.

Law

Lo (the Pidgin for law) has a wider connotation than its English counterpart. The dictionary defines law in its political sense as a rule of conduct or action prescribed by the supreme governing authority and enforced by a sanction, as any edict, decree, order, ordinance, statute, judicial decision, *etc*. However, *lo* has a broader meaning because it can mean not only *lo bilong gavman* (the law of the government), but also *lo bilong ol kanaka* (custom). According to a study, *lo* 'expresses and establishes religious, social and legal links within a group, over against other groups or in connection with ancestors and deities.'[28] Hence *lo* can be applied validly to activities ranging from etiquette (such as giving a betel nut to another person), to religious rituals, or to legal obligations between spouses and relatives.

Lo furthermore implies a mutual relationship between two parties to act reciprocally. The other side of the agreement may include not only the living, but even ancestors and deities who 'are called upon to safeguard the fulfillment of the *lo* even if they are not directly involved.'[29] Even if there may be no original Melanesian word for law, it can be translated as the 'way of life'.[30] In short, *lo* 'could be described as a system of religious, social and legal reciprocity.'[31]

Since the law concerns the relationship between two parties, the rights and duties of both parties come into play. It can also apply to the same person. For example, the right to marry also implies the duty of the person to support his family. Where the social philosophy enshrines the individual, human rights may be extolled as something absolute, but in the context of Melanesian social philosophy where the individual is a part of a group, the duty overshadows rights.

Western laws are like geometric principles which are to be applied to concrete situations. But since Melanesian logic is concrete and proceeds inductively, the law is also concrete and, in particular, interpersonal. Since harmony is one important mark of social philosophy, disagreements are often settled by some form of mutual compensation, which gives the semblance of having no winners. According to Narokobi, 'there is a notion of winning and losing in the legal system that we inherited...But the original Melanesian idea is of a no-win, no-lose justice.'[32]

Double standard justice seems to be a problem, at least as seen by an outsider. For example, if a great man and a commoner commit rape, the latter may be fined heavily but the former is not. But Mantovani claims that the case may not be double-standard in Melanesia:

> The big-man acquires his status through continual proof of his assistance to the community; his position is the acknowledgement by the members of the community of his great services to it. The lesser mortal is just that because the community has not experienced much help from such a person. He or she is useless ... The big-man has a very positive credit, so his harm is balanced by the good he keeps doing. The ordinary villager, on the other hand, harms the community without any hope of making good the damage he has done, and so is made to pay for his debt. There are not two standards, but only one: the well being of the community, and it is for that community to draw appropriate lines.[33]

Papua New Guinea (and perhaps the other Melanesian countries) have two legal systems: the traditional and the imported. The traditional legal philosophy is gradually being eroded by the system imposed by the colonial masters. The village courts still follow the spirit of the Melanesian legal philosophy but the higher courts follow the system imposed by Australia which, in turn, was copied from England. So, the local magistrates of the higher courts put on wigs, shirts, and shoes and follow the mentality of Western courts. But the village court judges go barefoot and follow the wisdom of their Melanesian ancestors. Those who lose in the lower courts appeal to the higher courts which often overturn the decision of the former. Thus Bernard Narokobi, who was chairman of the Law Reform Commission of Papua New Guinea, as well as a constitutional planner, decided cases according to Melanesian law. But some of them have been 'overruled by the supreme court.'[34]

Egoism existed before colonial times but was not protected by tradition. But now Westernised law protects egoism. The rich and the powerful have the law to protect their selfish interests. The law becomes a tool of the few to the detriment of the majority, as happened also in the Philippines.[35] John Momis[36] has made decisive contributions in giving a Melanesian flavour to the PNG constitution, but he has enemies who want to bend the constitution to their selfish motives.

The Independent State of Papua New Guinea promotes greed and selfishness ... We cannot talk about equitable distribution or sharing unless we take control of these mechanisms and reshape them to achieve the goals of our nation's founding fathers.[37]

Most of the Melanesian countries have just gained their independence. But they also inherited a legal system based on Western legal philosophy. As mentioned above, the system is biased to protect the powerful rich and will therefore hurt nation-building. Unless some enlightened leaders forget their vested interests and lead reforms according to Melanesian thinking, the future looks dark. But while the new countries are still malleable, there is still hope for reform.

IV. Philosophy of the unseen world

This section will deal with the Melanesian view of the world and with ethics.

Holistic worldview

We have seen that the Melanesian as individual does not dichotomise his faculties, but sees himself as a whole person. The same is true of the Melanesian worldview. All writers agree that the Melanesian does not have a dualistic concept of the other world. His Western counterpart thinks of reality as either profane or sacred, physical or spiritual, dead or alive. This distinction does not hold with the Melanesian who holds everything as integral.

Religion is not separate in life. The Melanesian's ultimate concern is life in its material, biological, and spiritual aspects and as it permeates everything. A shorter word for this is biocosmic. Salvation then for the Melanesian is also integral, as in the biblical term for peace (*shalom*). The all-comprising term in Pidgin is *gutpela sindaun*.[38]

It means fulfillment in every aspect of life, be it health, success, fertility, respect, honour, or influence over others. Ultimately it is the absence of such negative forces in life as sickness, death, defeat, infertility, contempt, or poverty.[39]

Connected with *gutpela sindaun* is *pawa* (power) or *strong* (strength) which is concerned with getting results. Since the Melanesian is pragmatic and a concrete thinker, he is concerned about attaining his *gutpela sindaun*. Therefore, he is not interested in what is profane and what is sacred; he is concerned with power and what is powerless. Power is not the same as holy. There are Melanesian words connected with power such as what places are to be avoided. A place is 'powerful' because it may house a special stone. Not everyone has access to the place because the stone can kill an unqualified person.

The spirits are important in the biocosmic worldview. Ancestors (both historical and mythical) and immanent spirits play a major role. One informant said that he always felt the presence of his departed father wherever he went. He felt reminded through ordinary creatures such as a bird or a firefly which appear in unusual places. If the Melanesian forgets his departed elders he becomes sick: sicknesses often are attributed to forgetting the departed. Hence the social philosophy of being in community applies not only to the visible but also to the invisible.

The Melanesian vision sees the human person in his totality with the spirit world, as well as the animal and plant worlds. This human person is not absolute master of the universe, but an important

Synkrētic

component in an interdependent world of person with animal, plant, and spirit.[40]

Ethics

Recent years have witnessed a rethinking of ethics and of moral theology.[41] If morality is based on human nature, there are cultural factors which are not universal and yet affect ethical judgment. One extreme rightist position is that some actions are always evil, while others are always good. The other, leftist, school claims that action are good or bad depending simply upon their results. To avoid both extreme positions, value ranking has been proposed as the basis of morality. We have already dealt with this matter elsewhere, and no elaboration is needed here.

Since Melanesia is in a state of change, its traditional values seemingly have been shaken. Traditional, Christian, and secular values have been competing in society.[42] As we have seen in the *wantok* system for example, there is change but at the same time cultural continuity.

In the Melanesian value ranking the foremost value is life.[43] As mentioned earlier, life is understood here in the context of *gutpela sindaun*, that is, in harmonious relationship with the community, with the ancestors, with the environment. In short, life is experienced as communal and cosmic. The second value is the community which includes the living and the departed. Third is the value of relationships (to one's community and other communities, to the ancestors, and to the whole environment). Fourth is the value of exchange which symbolises relationships.

Mantovani gives as an example of applied value ranking that, in traditional Simbu society, a twin baby was killed because the mother could not breast-feed two babies for the prescribed three years. Furthermore, malnutrition also existed and the rate of infant mortality is high. If it is hard for a single baby to survive in the bush, it is harder for two. 'Experience has taught society that both will slowly starve or die of some illness, and that by cutting the milk from one, the other has at least a 60 per cent chance of survival.'[44]

Another example is that of double standard which was explained above. In Melanesian society stealing in secret is traditionally all right; it becomes bad only when the thief's identity is known. This is so because in an area where property is communal, the value of relationship (which was broken by theft) is more important than the value of property.

Value ranking has to be more clarified as society changes. Thus, if better health comes to the community, the value of life may be translated in the case mentioned above as a shift from infanticide to family planning.

V. Conclusion

The foregoing has been a sketch of Melanesian philosophy. An important characteristic is its philosophy of 'being with' which colours the various aspects of Melanesian thought. As such Melanesian and Filipino philosophy have many things in common. However, this is not the place to point out the differences.

Since philosophical categories are important for theologising, Melanesian philosophy becomes a tool enabling the development of a Melanesian theology. The following are some areas where the categories may apply. Its social philosophy enables the Melanesian to understand more clearly the Mystical Body of Christ, that the departed and the present form one living reality as the Communion of Saints. Salvation as a holistic *gutpela sindaun*, together with the philosophy of time, points to realised eschatology. Likewise, the concrete Melanesian thinking may be applied to the theology of signs. Melanesian philosophy may also be applied to other fields. For example, it may help to rethink the reform of the colonial legal system in Melanesia.

It is not claimed that this analysis is final. Like the other social sciences, the findings of this philosophical study must remain tentative until disproven by more convincing data.

Synkrētic

Notes

1. Marie de Lepervanche, 'Social Structure', in *Anthropology in Papua New Guinea*, ed. Ian Hogbin (Carlton, Victoria: Melbourne University Press, 1973), 1-60.
2. *Bernard Narokobi* (1943-2010) was a prominent Papua New Guinean politician, legal reformer, philosopher, and Catholic who famously coined the concept of 'Melanesian Way'.
3. Bernard Narokobi, *The Melanesian Way*, rev. ed. (Boroko, PNG: Institute of Papua New Guinea Studies, 1983).
4. Frank Mihalic, *The Jacaranda Dictionary and Grammar of Melanesian Pidgin* (Milton, Queensland: The Jacaranda Press, 1971), 10.
5. Leonardo N. Mercado, *Elements of Filipino Philosophy* (Tacloban City: Divine Word University Publications, 1974).
6. Narokobi, *The Melanesian Way*, 185.
7. Mercado, *Elements of Filipino Philosophy*, 3-48.
8. Tables 10 and 11 are not reproduced in this excerpt and are available in the original text. See Leonardo N. Mercado, *The Filipino Mind: Philippine Philosophical Studies II* (Washington, D.C.: Council for Research in Values and Philosophy, 1994).
9. *Tokbokis*: a Pidgin word for 'parable' or 'secret language'.
10. See Leonardo N. Mercado, 'On snow and the Filipino mind', in *Synkrētic*, №1 (Feb. 2022): 99-102.
11. Darell Whiteman, 'Melanesian Religions: An Overview', in *An Introduction to Melanesian Religions*, ed. Ennio Mantovani (Goroka: The Melanesian Institute, 1984), 93.
12. Mercado, *Elements of Filipino Philosophy*, 82-89.
13. M. John Paul Chao, 'Leadership', in *An Introduction to Melanesian Cultures*, ed. Darrell L. Whiteman (Goroka: The Melanesian Institute, 1984), 127.
14. Brian Schwarz, 'Urbanisation', in *An Introduction to Melanesian Cultures*, 238-240.
15. Mary McDonald, 'Melanesian Communities: Past and Present', in *An Introduction to Melanesian Cultures*, 221.
16. *Ibid.*, 217.
17. Narokobi, *The Melanesian Way*, 13.
18. Mihalic, *The Jacaranda Dictionary*, 28.
19. *Ibid.*, 29.
20. Mantovani, personal communication, 8 February 1988.
21. William Ross, 'Grammar of the Mogei Language' (typescript, n.d.), 29.
22. David Vincent, personal communication, 8 February 1988.
23. Mercado, *Elements of Filipino Philosophy*, 111-115.

24 Kev Hovey, 'Towards Effective Ministry in Endemic Cargo Areas', in *Religious Movements in Melanesia Today* (2), ed. Wendy Flannery (Goroka: The Melanesian Institute), 119-121.
25 Mihalic, *The Jacaranda Dictionary*, 123.
26 Mercado, *Elements of Filipino Philosophy*, 145.
27 Bernard Narokobi, 'The Old and the New', in *Ethics and Development in Papua New Guinea*, ed. Gernot Fugmann (Goroka: The Melanesian Institute, 1986), 10-14.
28 Gernot Fugman, 'Salvation Expressed in a Melanesian Context', in *Christ in Melanesia* (Goroka: The Melanesian Institute, 1977), 124.
29 *Loc. cit.*
30 Narokobi, 'The Old and the New', 7.
31 Gernot Fugmann, 'Salvation in Melanesian Religions', in *An Introduction to Melanesian Religions*, 287.
32 Narokobi, 'The Old and the New', 8.
33 Mantovani, 'Traditional Values and Ethics', 207-208.
34 Narokobi, 'The Old and the New', 15.
35 Leonardo N. Mercado, *Legal Philosophy: Western, Eastern, and Filipino* (Tacloban City: Divine Word University Publications, 1984).
36 *John Momis*: a former Catholic priest and politician who drafted Papua New Guinea's constitution from 1972 to 1975 and who became President of the Autonomous Region of Bougainville from 2010 to 2020.
37 Narokobi, 'The Old and the New', 15.
38 See George Mombi, 'The Melanesian concept of *gutpela sindaun*', in *Synkrētic*, №1 (Feb. 2022): 34-45.
39 Fugmann, 'Salvation in Melanesian Religions', 282.
40 Narokobi, *The Melanesian Way*, 6.
41 Leonardo N. Mercado, *Elements of Filipino Ethics* (Tacloban City: Divine Word University Publications, 1979), 13-43.
42 Garry Trompf, 'Competing Value-Orientation in Papua New Guinea', in *Ethics and Development in Papua New Guinea*, 17-34; William Edoni, 'The Confrontation of Traditional and Christian Values in Papua New Guinea', *Ibid.*, 35-42. In both articles the authors mean Christian values as espoused by the imported westernised Christianity. But if Christianity is to be inculturated, there will be no great conflict between Christian and traditional values.
43 Mantovani, 'Traditional Values and Ethics'.
44 *Ibid.*, 209.

The pattern for a good life: Indigenous Solomon Islands ethics

Kabini Sanga*
Martyn Reynolds[†]

Ethics is a field that can be subject to unwarranted universality. Nonetheless, ethics is complex and subject to place-based specificity. In this article, we show through examples how Indigenous Solomon Islands ethics expresses group identity, structures collective intergenerational coherence, supports the productive navigation of new contexts, and provides a plank for the building of much-needed nationhood. Our aims are to provide food for thought to a wider audience regarding the way ethics is understood, discussed, and enacted, to honour the originators and practitioners of Indigenous Solomon Islands ethical systems, and to assert their value as a pattern for a good life.

Ethics

Defining ethics is hard and can feel like 'nailing jello to a wall'.[1] While the term 'ethics' may be accepted as referring to the codification of what is right and wrong, rightness and wrongness are contextual and a matter of subjectivity. In this essay, we look at eth-

---

* Kabini Sanga is Associate Professor of Education at the University of Wellington. He holds a PhD from the University of Saskatchewan and lives in Wellington, New Zealand.
† Martyn Reynolds is Pacific Education Research Postdoctoral Fellow at Victoria University of Wellington (VUW). He holds a PhD from VUW and lives in Wellington, New Zealand.

ics and social sustainability in Solomon Islands, an enterprise worthwhile for at least three reasons.

Firstly, the specifics of ethics offer a salutary lesson to participants in fields such as educational research, in which a tendency to impose the ethics of one group upon another is evident.

Secondly, since multiple voices are helpful in appreciating new possibilities, discussion of Indigenous Solomon Islands ethics may offer wisdom of value in wider contexts.

Thirdly and most importantly, exploring Indigenous Solomon Islands ethics brings honour to the originators and practitioners of Solomon Islands Indigenous ethical systems, asserting the strength of Indigenous Solomon Islands societies as self-sustaining and able to cope with change by understanding the pattern for a good life on their own terms.

In order to present our exploration, which draws on earlier research,[2] the narrative begins by eroding universalistic approaches to ethics. We then turn to ethics as an element of collective identity for the Gwailao clan from East Mala'ita, Solomon Islands. This theme is further developed through a research-based account of ethical education as a means to collective intergenerational coherence that describes how ethics are transmitted and reinforced amongst children and adults at the clan and village level. What follows next is a detailed examination of the relationship between ethical principles and change in the context of a *rara'aba* (a calming of nerves meeting). Finally, adopting a wider Solomon Islands nation-state lens, we consider the potential of school-based Solomon Islands citizenship education founded on the ethical responsibilities of being a *wantok* (literally a person who speaks the same language) through the work of Billy Fito'o.[3]

The ethics of specifics

Many global and Pacific voices have noted the way ethics have been imposed through research on Indigenous peoples. Linda Tuhiwai Smith, for example, notes how unequal power relationships between researchers and Indigenous peoples result in Indigenous

Synkrētic

individuals and groups becoming the subjects of research, made exotic in the process.[4] In the context of Solomon Islands research, we have shown that a shift towards research partnerships between non-Indigenous and Indigenous Solomon Islanders has been slow, and that very little research has been framed in *kastom* (customary) terms.[5] It is unsurprising, therefore, to find that a systematic neglect by research ethics committees of collective rights and community consent[6] has resulted in the assertion of a Western-biased ethical system that assumes individual rights to be paramount.[7]

Under the guise of universalism, inappropriate ethical codes have therefore been applied when researching Indigenous knowledge.[8] This has led to the disenfranchisement of Indigenous ethical processes[9] and unethical encroachment on the knowledge systems of Indigenous peoples.[10] Evidence from the Pacific of these issues includes the questioning of the cultural validity of ethical decisions made by professional and university research organisations,[11] the imposition of potentially misplaced ethical principles such as autonomy, beneficence, and non-maleficence,[12] and the inappropriateness of non-Indigenous ethical frameworks to capture unstated Indigenous knowledge.[13]

Two immediate challenges arise from this situation.

First, Indigenous peoples are challenged to reclaim their Indigenous knowledge and ethical systems from the exoticised positions to which these have been relegated in and by the academy, establishing their rightful places within a global knowledge economy. In the Oceania region, the taking up of this challenge can be seen in the works of Māori[14] and Islander scholars.[15]

Second, there is a challenge to Western research institutions to recognise the value, contributions, and legitimacy of Indigenous knowledge systems and to negotiate research approaches that are ethically appropriate, dignified, and respectful and which honour the wisdoms of all those who are involved.

This article makes contributions in both areas. We unequivocally assert the value of Solomon Islands ethical systems as complete and effective in their own right to describe and support the patterns of a good life in context. We do this by providing specific examples, making visible to the academy those things which should be valued in research (and other fields), thereby providing both the matter and model for honourable encounters. In writing this paper, Kabini could be described as an 'insider' researcher, being a Gula'alā person of the Gwailao clan who acknowledges personal responsibility for any limitations of description, interpretation, or execution of this new area of Indigenous Oceania scholarship. Martyn could be described as an 'outsider' researcher whose role has been to provide a sounding board to support the construction of discussion. We advance this scholarship through our relationship, understanding matters of inside/outside to be relational,[16] focused from our different socialisations and perspectives on a common good which we both embrace.

Solomon Islands

Diversity characterises the Solomon Islands. An archipelago of over 900 islands, Solomon Islands lies between Papua New Guinea to the west and Vanuatu to the southeast. Although the term 'Melanesian' is often applied to the Solomon Islands population, some groups who reside there have ancestral links to Polynesian and Micronesian groups. Around 80 languages are spoken and multiple cultural groups make up the nation-state.[17] Pijin, a Melanesian creole,[18] provides mutual intelligibility across Solomon Islands and within Melanesia as a whole. English is the official language, a consequence of Solomon Islands' status as a British Protectorate prior to independence in 1978. Honiara on the island of Guadalcanal is the capital. Few other urban settlements exist, although Auki, the provincial capital of Mala'ita province, is one.

Solomon Islanders generally recognise three domains of influence. Formal institutional life is a domain that includes government bodies, systems such as formal education, and diverse other statutory bodies and activities. The church domain is focussed on the many Christian denominations that form part of the social fabric. *Kastom* is the domain of practices and understandings that are customary, well-understood, and tested by time. The three domains

Synkrētic

compete for influence but are generally thought of as significant in ascending order as listed.[19] Consequently, *kastom* ethics are influential across domain borders, and activities in the formal domain such as school leadership or research are unlikely to profit from running counter to *kastom*.[20] Thus, we pay attention to *kastom* ethics through the example of the Gwailao clan from East Mala'ita as an example of ethics as a contributor to identity.

The Gula'alā of Mala'ita

Mala'ita Island is the most populated part of the Solomon Islands archipelago. It is rugged and mountainous with dense tropical forests, deep harbours, and has lagoons in the west, southwest, and northeast. The island is divided culturally and linguistically into Toabaita, Baelelea, Baegu, Lau, Fataleka, Kwara'ae, Langalanga, Kwaio, Dorio, 'Are'Are, Sa'a, and Gula'alā. Anthropologically speaking, Mala'ita cultures are patrilineal and egalitarian, although clan groups in 'Are'Are and Sa' embrace a more structured chiefly system.

The linguistic group which we describe is the Gula'alā, an Indigenous people at home on the east coast of Mala'ita Island. The Gula'alā are made up of seven clan groups, all of whom speak the Gula'alā language, one of twelve linguistic entities on Mala'ita Island. The Gula'alā number 1,800 people and live in seven villages in the Kwai and Uru harbours of east Mala'ita. Although their ancestral religion is a form of animism, the Gula'alā are now Christians. Gula'alā people continue to live a subsistence lifestyle, following customs and ethics of communitarianism. The Gula'alā clan of interest here is Gwailao. Gwailao understandings, ethics, and practices are rendered through Gula'alā terms.[21]

Ethics and identity in Mala'ita

Mala'ita tribes are theocratic and ruled by priests. The tribes' Indigenous religious system involves paying homage to ancestors' spirits. As in other Melanesian societies, Mala'ita tribes are socially egalitarian, with no clear hierarchical chiefly system. Instead, the *fata'abu baita* (high priest) oversees the tribe's affairs. Other spiritual (*wane foa*), civic (*aofia / alafa*), and war (*ramo*) leaders exist in Mala'ita tribal settings. However, among the Gula'alā, the *fata'abu* holds most power over certain things and people. Under Christianity, the majority of Mala'ita tribes do not have practising *fata'abu*. Exceptions include communities in Kwaio, Baeg[1], and the Lau regions. The absence of *fata'abu* rule, however, has not restricted the influence of Indigenous Mala'ita. Each tribe is an integrated community, with daily living and the sense of a good life primarily anchored in the tribal theocratic belief system.

The Indigenous Mala'ita ethical system is living. Tribes as *kastom* collectives and as contemporary communities are organised through complex sets of *tagi* (Gula'alā for a system of morality), categories, and levels of conventions, laws, benchmarks, and associated processes. These separate right from wrong and good from bad, and frame rewards and punishments. Mala'ita society has clear dispositions and seeks to influence its members to behave accordingly. Tribal groups in Mala'ita have specific character traits for resolving moral dilemmas and cultivating virtue. Today, this ethical system operates daily with and beyond the systems of a nation-state, Westminster democracy, as well as multiple Christian denominations. Since each tribal unit is enmeshed with its religious system, there is a high level of integration between socio-economic, political, ethical, and religious worlds which overlap into a single whole. Consequently, being good or bad and doing well or doing ill has the potential to affect the survival or death of the tribe. Morality is directly linked to Mala'ita belief systems. These are not just human and physical but spiritual, and metaphysical as well.[22] Unethical conduct by a member of a tribe can be fatal for the entire collective.

Integration is a key feature of Mala'ita ethics. In Mala'ita society, there is an overlapping relationship between personal and societal ethics such that private and communal morality are indistinct. Often, communal tribal ethics mandate and obligate the ethics of individuals. The privileging of the group reflects Mala'ita ontological, epistemological, cosmological, and axiological assumptions about nature.[23] The Mala'ita individual is a principal vehicle of rep-

Synkrētic

resentation for the tribe; one is not dialectically opposed to the other.

In Indigenous Mala'ita ethics, *abu* (holiness, also *tapu* in some Polynesian societies) is a unifying principle. *Abu* is the glue that binds the Indigenous Mala'ita ethical system together, is the culmination of integrity, and is a central normative piece in Mala'ita ethics.[24] *Abu* refers to being set apart in behaviour, action, and worship. It reflects goodness, rightness, and credibility to honour horizontally and vertically. *Abu* mediates and measures what is deemed fair, correct, and just. *Abu* explains the state of relationships, protocols and spaces of purpose, connection, and separation between tribe members and their neighbours in the natural world. *Abu* places constraints on humans to stop them being 'bad' and mediates against absolute power or the abuse of power. Through restraint, *abu* points people to spirit-gods or God. In Mala'ita cosmology, *abu* compels people to relate to others as co-dependents in a complex, wide, and holistic universe.

Indigenous Mala'ita ethics privileges the principle of *rō lā* (obedience) more than other significant values. In theocratic Mala'ita, *rō lā* is worship, a means of submission and demonstrating loyalty to the other, particularly to authority. This is because to be obedient is right doing. Particularly when loyalty to spirit-gods is at issue, obedient action by a clan member is an ethical outcome. The Indigenous Mala'ita ethical system does not privilege other important principles. If obedience to tribal interest is weighed against fairness, obedience as loyalty is privileged over fairness. The privileging of obedience over fairness explains the old *kastom* 'random' killing of individuals, the powerful conversions to Christianity that have occurred, and the desecration though not discarding of tribal shrines by former tribal members who have become Christians.

To summarise, an Indigenous Mala'ita ethics such as that of the Gula'alā is an integrated social-economic-political-religious system, a key aspect of collective identity. Mala'ita people's theocratic orientation means that Indigenous ethics is fundamentally linked to the tribal religion. The underpinning understandings of this system of ethics suggest that Mala'ita ethics is predominantly deontological, with aspects of teleological and virtue-based ethics.

Ethics and intergenerational coherence

The transmission of ethics to support intergenerational coherence can be explored in the Gula'alā context by drawing on different data sources.[25] These include *sili* (creative genres by expert knowledge-holders which are spoken or sung); *fānanaua* (specific teachings, intended to shape character); *fānanau lā 'inatō* (concentrated teachings on ethics, usually focusing on key principles or virtues) and *alā lā kini* (intentional, focused discussions) with expert knowledge guardians. We give examples of these forms in practice.[26]

Ethics education in Gula'alā starts early. For example, an adult might sing a *sili* about an admired ancestor. When performed for a group of youth, the *sili* exalts the ancestor and provides a moral compass:

> *'Oe 'o adomia ai 'oro* (You, a helper of many)
> *Ai ana malutā* (A cultured one)
> *Ai nē 'e kwaimani* (A loving one)
> *Ai nē 'e 'abero* (A caring one)
> *Ai 'e aroaro* (A peaceful one)
> *Ai 'e rō* (The obedient one)
> *Ai 'o manata sulia ta rau 'oko adea fana toa*
> (One who instigates plans to serve people).

Fānanau lā (ethics education) sessions for adolescent boys might address restraint behaviour; obedience to or respect for adults; industriousness or willingness to participate; the honouring of or respect for women and girls; the honouring of and respect for clan sisters; the importance of openness about girls of interest; care for widows and or orphans; and truthfulness in life in general.

Faānanau lā for girls might focus on personal character and relationships:

Synkrētic

> *Rarī nau 'ae, kosi leka 'i rara tei fili 'oe. 'Oe leka nō mone 'abitana tē 'oe.*
> (My daughter, in undertaking your food gathering chores in the garden, ensure you're accompanied by and traveling in your mother's shadows.)

> *'Oe ai ana madakwa lā, 'o gonia rau 'oe kini fāsia tō tatagafolo lā.*
> (You, a girl of the light, keep your domestic tools/equipment together. Never live untidily.)

> *'Oe wela geni rari, kosi gouru siana maiwane 'oe.*
> (You, an adolescent girl, never sit together with your brother.)[27]

In addition, ethics education includes *abu la* (holiness). Examples of girls being ethically socialised to keep themselves pure include:

> *Rarī nau 'ae, 'oe goni tei 'oe. 'oe abutai 'oe.*
> (My daughter, keep yourself contained. Keep yourself holy.)

And:

> *'Oe wela geni fi baita, fāsia tō nuinui lā.*
> (You, an adolescent girl, are not to live uncleanly.)[28]

For Gula'alā, cleanliness extends beyond the physical to embrace a spiritual state of well-being and discipline.

For both boys and girls in their teenage years, *fānanau lā* can deal with the shaping of character, citizenship, and the promotion of virtuous living, expressed across a range of topics. These include promise-keeping, transparency, generosity, and blamelessness:

> *Fata alangai lā rau baita. Alangai ko adea mala ta rau.*
> (Promise-keeping is a big deal. A promise made must always be kept.)

> *Na wela mamana 'e ade madakwa ana rau nia kini.*
> (A credible child is transparent in their deeds.)

> *'O sasae fana fanga lea la ana kwatea 'oe kini.*
> (Learn to be generous/open-handed/hospitable with your gifts/blessings/privileges.)

> *'O tō, adea ta maefatā ka toe 'oe nā.*
> (Live your life above reproach, beyond the reach of verbal attacks.)[29]

Indigenous Solomon Islands ethics

Ethics education does not stop at children, however. Ethical continuity and coherence are reinforced in teaching such as through *fānanau lā* for adults. Men may be encouraged to listen as leaders, be morally upright and honouring to their wives. Examples of *fānanau lā* subject matter recorded for women include restraint in speech and child discipline, and honourable relationships with in-laws. Sanga recorded instances of *fānanau lā* to men and women that emphasised character reshaping in contexts such as forgiveness and wisdom:

Maea 'e masi 'oe, leka 'oe kosi raufanatā ana ta wane 'amoe ko ogarasu ma'amu. Wane mamana kasi fali ma'ana fana maea.
(The end of the road of unforgiveness and anger is death. A person of character does not walk to his/her death.)

'O rongo, ko ada ma ko fali ana kali'afu lā. Bōngia luma 'oe ana liotō lā.
(Listen, look, and walk wholesomely. Set the foundation of your family with wisdom.)[30]

Ethics education is particularly significant for Gula'alā because of the collective nature of clan life and thought. Within the holistic and integrated social-economic-political-religious system, identity is collective as much as it is individual, and coherence supports sustainability across generations. This means that the young need to be socialised into clan ethics and adults need to be guided to remain consistent in their ethical practice. Adults who fail in this are likely to be ineffectual in supporting new generations to learn appropriately because modelling appropriate character-shaped behaviour itself has educative outcomes. Since the action of the individual affects collective wellbeing, the consistent ethical behaviour of one is a benefit to all.

Ethics and change

The Mala'ita ethical system is living and therefore equipped to cope with changed circumstances. Political change has visited Solomon Islands in the form of inter-ethnic strife.[31] Climate change is also a vital issue.[32] Here, we turn to how Mala'ita ethics mediate technolo-

Synkrētic

gical change in the form of the publication of a book of clan knowledge.³³

In Mala'ita society, three kinds of knowledge can be identified. We have argued that public knowledge is available to almost everyone.³⁴ This includes knowledge about food, farming, fishing, and some medicinal information and is knowledge required for daily survival. *Faka* (introduced) knowledge, learned in school, from the media, or the Church is also deemed public.

Specialised knowledge such as some medicinal or some trade knowledge (as used by master fishermen or hunters), some social-spiritual knowledge (relevant to secret societies and sorcerers), and all clan genealogical knowledge falls into this category in Mala'ita. Such knowledge can be held by secret societies or coded in secret language so that access is restricted. A certain kind of qualification is needed to gain entry. One aim of restricting secret specialised knowledge is to maintain its purity and power.

A third category is sacred knowledge. This is about the day-to-day but maintains spatial and temporal links with spiritual dimensions in time and beyond.³⁵ Sacred knowledge preserves spiritual continuity within the theocratic clan structure of Mala'ita. The names of clan-tribal ancestor spirits, physical, and verbal forms of knowledge repositories that are associated with tribal religious ceremonies and certain ritualistic utterances or invocations are examples. The category also includes that which sustains holy living and uprightness of moral character. Access is limited to those who are qualified so that the sanctity of the knowledge is maintained.

When knowledge is organised in these ways, ethical issues surround the boundaries of knowledge and its access. The publication of *Fānanau lā i Gula'alā*,³⁶ a book of secret and sacred Gwailao clan knowledge rendered in the Gula'alā language, provided an opportunity to see the clan mediate between apparently contradictory ethical principles: technological change in the form of the book on the one hand and social change in the form of migration away from the village on the other. In effect, the *rara'aba* (calming of nerves meeting) that provided resolution addressed the ethics of the movement of knowledge between domains.

In communitarian Mala'ita, a person's identity can be both individual ('I') and communal ('We'). Consequently, when an individual plays the role of exercising the ethics of knowledge guardianship, they act as an individual and as a family or clan representative. Two principles exercised in the *rara'aba* show how ethics in Indigenous Mala'ita knowledge responds to change.

The principle of *'ado lā ana rau lea fainia tōa* or stewardship promotes the value of sharing good things with others. Since knowledge is assumed to be good, it is worth sharing now and in the future. Knowledge guardians have ethical responsibilities to care for the content and status of the knowledge. In addition, *'ado lā* or stewardship operates through *nao-nao lā* or seniority. Thus, ethical questions in the matter of the publication of *Fānanau lā i Gula'alā* invoked decisions that appreciate guardianship in relation to the knowledge, and sensitivity about a speaker's position in relation to others. The *rara'aba* was intended to develop these understandings.

Seniority in Gula'alā can be a complex matter that includes the examples of *garangi*, guardianship vested by virtue of a direct line to the first custodian of the knowledge; gender and age such as through *futa lā* and *wane ma geni*; and blood relations as in *futa lā ana tē 'abu*. We discuss other forms of seniority elsewhere.[37] Dimensions of seniority might seem fixed, but the strength of Mala'ita ethics is revealed by the fluid negotiation possible when faced with innovative circumstances such as the production of a book of restricted knowledge.

During the *rara'aba*, secrecy itself was not at issue. Debate addressed the nature and scope of secrecy. A time-based thread presented opportunities to examine how the origin of the knowledge in question affected its secrecy. Genealogical questions were asked to probe where and when the originator obtained the knowledge, drawing attention to the way transmission occurs through clan structures and extending to prior generations the parameters of secrecy. In this way, the *rara'aba* eroded unequivocal claims about the type and level of secrecy relevant.

In addition, the movement of knowledge through space was discussed. For example, women bring knowledge to a clan through

Synkrētic

marriage. Consequently, the origin and distribution patterns of secret knowledge are less clear than might be assumed. An ethical question relevant here is whether knowledge is held in expressions of wisdom or the teaching that the wisdom embodies. If embodied wisdom is visible, the boundaries of secrecy are more inclusive than exclusive. As a result, further transfer is possible by learning through action. Thus, secrecy may not be as intense as some might think, and the status of immediate guardianship deserves reconsideration. Interrogating knowledge transfer through space questions the relevance of certain principles of seniority since the way people relate to knowledge deemed secret is not always predictable.

The application of principles of knowledge guardianship in the *rara'aba* reveals much about Indigenous Solomon Islands ethics. First, ethics involves the application of known and agreed principles, but complex situations require sifting through principles to arrive at a conclusion. Indigenous Solomon Islands ethics for the Gula'alā are not absolute but contextual. In the *rara'aba*, clan members' intersecting contributions resulted in a decision by and on behalf of the clan through peeling back layers of the ethics of the context to reveal the quality, intensity, and significance of secrecy.

In the case of the publication of *Fānanau lā 'I Gula'alā*, the ethics of both secrecy and decision-making led to the book being published for the education of future generations, since the transfer and therefore existence of the knowledge was deemed more significant than its secrecy and the role of guardians in preserving this. By negotiating ethical principles to meet the new circumstances of publication technology and migration away from the village, unity was preserved by the *rara'aba* process and sustainability protected by its decision.

Ethics and nationhood

Solomon Islands is a multi-ethnic nation state. Formal education is largely centralised and administered from Honiara. School teachers may find themselves in ethical dilemmas when Indigenous ethics seem to be contradicted by policy or practice.[38] Given the recent history of inter-ethnic tensions, it is important for nation-building that Indigenous Solomon Islands ethics inform the citizenship curriculum. One way to achieve this is to develop a curriculum of *wantok*-framed citizenship.[39]

Taken literally, a *wantok* is a person who speaks the same language. Paliaima Aiyery Tanda explains that the 'wantok system is a relationship of sharing, supporting, protecting, providing, and caring that reaches out to meet the needs, wants, and desires of individuals and groups, who are related. It is a system that focuses on maintaining kinship relations . . .'.[40]

Fangalea writes of 'a system that places high value on people, related biologically, linguistically, culturally, and regionally'.[41] Originally centred on language groupings, discussion of being a *wantok* has extended to fields such as sport,[42] religion,[43] and resilience in the face of natural disasters.[44] While some see wantokism as primarily negative and associate it with corruption,[45] being a *wantok* involves ethics of reciprocation and care that are relational strengths associated with the communitarian understandings that a person's identity can be both individual ('I') and communal ('We'), and that the benefit of the group and the protection of the collective are everyone's responsibility.

Fito'o argues that a 'wantok-centred framework for understanding citizenship is significant for the stability of the Solomon Islands; it draws from Indigenous cultures, modern democracy, and Christianity as guiding principles'.[46] This is particularly true in a context where, unlike in Western societies, citizenship is understood through morality and spirituality, reflecting indigenous ethics and theocratic traditions. Fito'o found that Solomon Islanders' ideas of citizenship included people's engagement with communal activities such as sharing, working together, providing security, caregiving, ethical leadership, and peace-making.

A *wantok*-framed citizenship curriculum recognises these ideas of citizenship and places the ethics of coherent relationality as a core way to strengthen Solomon Islands citizenship through local beliefs, values, and aspiration. In ways that are congruent with the three domains of influence that we have ascribed to the Melanesian

Synkrētic

mind,⁴⁷ the framework developed by Fito'o recognises that culture (*kastom*), spirituality (church), and modern institutions (institutional) are aspects of life that should be complementary. This is because they are inter-related, simultaneous and affect people in varying ways. *Kastom* may hold sway if these domains are placed in competition, but at the nation-state level the ethics of democracy derived from politics and law must negotiate productively with the relational and emotional values of the church and the relational ethics of *kastom*. In this way, a balance may be struck between the ethics of legal rights and *wantok*-framed responsibilities. The significance of Indigenous Solomon Islands ethics to *wantok*-centred citizenship is a base for the development of the nation-state founded not on top-down introduced thinking, but on Indigenous appreciations of life focussed on the well-understood ethics of being a *wantok*.

Conclusion

Diversity is a hallmark of Solomon Islands. Consequently, this article has provided a limited snapshot of Indigenous Solomon Islands ethics. We have attended to the way ethics contributes to collective identity for the Gula'alā, illustrated some ways the Gula'alā maintain intergenerational coherence through the transmission of ethical understandings, provided a window into how ethical principles are negotiated to productively navigate change, and pointed to the way Indigenous relational ethics can compete through citizenship education at the nation-state level. All these aspects of the discussion undercut universalist approaches to ethics and add nuance to notions of contextualisation for those such as educators, development professionals, and researchers who wish to benefit Solomon Islanders.⁴⁸ Indigenous Solomon Islands ethics provide a pattern for a good life lived in sustainable, communal, and peaceful ways. Since sustainability, unity, and peace sometimes seem in short supply at the global level, there is scope to honour those who have developed Indigenous ethics over millennia by seeking to learn from their values and practices.

Notes

1. P.V. Lewis, 'Defining "business ethics": Like nailing jello to a wall', in *Journal of Business Ethics*, Vol. 4, Issue 5 (1985): 377.

2. See Kabini Sanga, 'A first look at an Indigenous Pacific ethical system and its implications for research', in *Of Waves, Winds and Wonderful Things: A Decade of Rethinking Pacific Education*, eds. Mo'ale 'Otunuku, Unaisi Nabobo-Baba, and Seu'ula Johansson Fua (Nuku'alofa: Institute of Education, The University of the South Pacific, 2021): 148-160; Kabini Sanga, 'Ethics curriculum in indigenous pacific: A Solomon Islands study', in *AlterNative: An International Journal of Indigenous Peoples*, Vol. 15, Issue 3 (2019), 243-252; Kabini Sanga and Martyn Reynolds, 'Knowledge guardianship, custodianship and ethics: a Melanesian perspective', in *AlterNative*, Vol. 16, Issue 2 (2020): 99-107.

3. Billy Fito'o, 'Wantok-centred framework for developing citizenship', in *International Education Journal: Comparative Perspectives*, Vol. 18, Issue 2 (2019): 55-67.

4. Linda Tuhiwai Smith, *Decolonizing Methodologies: Research and Indigenous Peoples* (London: Zed Books, 1999).

5. Kabini Sanga and Martyn Reynolds, 'Waka hem no finis yet: Solomon Islands research futures', in *Pacific Dynamics*, Vol. 6, Issue 1 (2022): 30-49.

6. Kathleen Cranley Glass and Joseph Kaufert, 'Research Ethics Review and Aboriginal Community Values: Can the Two Be Reconciled?', in *Journal of Empirical Research on Human Research Ethics*, Vol. 2, Issue 2 (2007): 25-40.

7. Angela Brew, *The Nature of Research: Inquiry into academic contexts* (London: Routledge Falmer, 2001).

8. Marlene Brant Castellano, 'Ethics of Aboriginal Research', in *Journal of Aboriginal Health*, Vol. 1, No. 1 (Jan. 2004): 98-114.

9. Gus Worby and Daryle Rigney, 'Approaching ethical issues: Institutional management of indigenous research, in *Australian Universities Review*, Vol. 45, Issue 1 (2002): 24-33.

10. Ian Maddocks, 'Ethics in Aboriginal research: A model for minorities or for all?', in *Medical Journal of Australia*, Vol. 157, No. 8 (1992): 553-555.

11. Hirini Moko Mead, *Tikanga Māori: Living by Māori Values* (Wellington: Huia Publishers, 2003).

12. Māui Hudson, 'A Māori perspective on ethical review in health', paper presented at the Traditional Knowledge and Research Ethics conference, Ngā Pae O te Maramatanga, University of Auckland, 2005.

13. Kabini Sanga, 'The ethics of researching unstated contextual knowledge', in *Are theories universal?*, eds. Anders Örtenblad, Ibrahim Ahmad Bajunid, Muhammad Babur, and Roshmi Kumari (Kuala Lumpur: Yayasan Ilmuwan, 2011).

14. See *inter alia* Smith, *Decolonizing Methodologies*; Russell Bishop, 'Freeing ourselves from neo-colonial domination in research: A Māori approach to creating knowledge', in *Qualitative Studies in Education*, Vol. 11, Issue 2 (1998): 199-219.

15 David W. Gegeo, 'Indigenous knowledge and empowerment: Rural development examined from within', in *The Contemporary Pacific*, Vol. 10, No. 2 (Fall 1998): 289-315; Unaisi Nabobo-Baba, 'Fijian epistemology: Examining aspects of Vugalei cultural pedagogies, processes and possible futures', in *Re-thinking education curricula in the Pacific: Challenges and prospects*, eds. Kabini Sanga and Konai Helu Thaman (Wellington, NZ: He Parekereke Institute for Research and Development in Maori and Pacific Education, Victoria University of Wellington, 2008), 137-158.

16 Talitiga Ian Fasavalu and Martyn Reynolds, 'Relational positionality and a learning disposition: Shifting the conversation', in *International Education Journal: Comparative Perspectives*, Vol. 18, Issue 2 (2019): 11-25.

17 Sinclair Dinnen, 'Winners and losers: Politics and disorder in the Solomon Islands 2000-2002, in *Journal of Pacific History*, Vol. 37, Issue 3 (2002), 285-298.

18 Christine Jourdan and Johanne Angeli, 'Pijin and shifting language ideologies in urban Solomon Islands', in *Language in Society*, Vol. 43, Issue 3 (2014): 265-285.

19 Kabini Sanga and Martyn Reynolds, 'Melanesian tok stori in leadership development: Ontological and relational implications for donor-funded programmes in the Western Pacific', in *International Education Journal: Comparative Perspectives*, Vol. 17, Issue 4 (2019): 11-26.

20 Kabini Sanga, Seu'ula Johansson-Fua, Martyn Reynolds, David Fa'avae, Richard Robyns and Danny Jim, 'Getting beneath the skin': A *tok stori* approach to reviewing the literature of leadership in Solomon Islands, Tonga and Marshall Islands', in *International Education Journal: Comparative Perspectives*, Vol. 20, No. 2 (2021): 52-75.

21 Sanga, 'Ethics curriculum in indigenous pacific'.

22 Kabini Sanga and Keith Walker, 'The Malaitan mind and teamship: Implications of Indigenous knowledge for team development and performance', in *International Journal of Knowledge, Culture & Change Management*, Vol. 11, Issue 6 (2012): 223-235.

23 Sanga and Walker, 'The Malaitan mind and teamship'.

24 Sanga and Walker, 'The Malaitan mind and teamship'.

25 Sanga, 'A first look at an Indigenous Pacific ethical system and its implications for research'.

26 Sanga, 'A first look at an Indigenous Pacific ethical system and its implications for research'.

27 Sanga, 'A first look at an Indigenous Pacific ethical system and its implications for research'.

28 Sanga, 'A first look at an Indigenous Pacific ethical system and its implications for research'.

29 Sanga, 'A first look at an Indigenous Pacific ethical system and its implications for research'.

30 Sanga, 'A first look at an Indigenous Pacific ethical system and its implications for research'.

31 Matthew Allen (ed.), *Greed and Grievance: Ex-militants' Perspectives on the Conflict in Solomon Islands, 1998-2003* (Honolulu: University of Hawai'i Press, 2013); Shahar

Hameiri, 'The trouble with RAMSI: Reexamining the roots of conflict in Solomon Islands', in *The Contemporary Pacific*, Vol. 19, Issue 2 (2007): 409-441; Sherrill Whittington, Sofi Ospina and Alice Aruhe'eta Pollard, *Women in Government in Solomon Islands: A Diagnostic Study*, October 2006.

32 Ioan Fazey, Nathalie Pettorelli, Jasper Kenter, Daniel Wagatora and Daniel Schuett, 'Maladaptive trajectories of change in Makira, Solomon Islands, in *Global Environmental Change*, Vol. 21, Issue 4 (2011): 1275-1289; Douglas M. Rearic, *Coastal environment of Kwai and Ngongosila Islands, Malaita Province, Solomon Islands*, SOPAC technical report 121 (Suva: South Pacific Applied Geoscience Commission, 1991); Jan van der Ploeg, Meshach Sukulu, Hugh Govan, Tessa Minter, Hampus Eriksson, 'Sinking islands, drowned logic; climate change and community-based adaptation discourses in Solomon Islands', in *Sustainability*, Vol. 12, Issue 17 (2020): 1-23; Kabini Sanga, *Fānanau lā i Gula'alā* (Wellington: TNR Literatures, 2014).

33 Sanga and Reynolds, 'Knowledge guardianship, custodianship and ethics'.

34 Sanga and Reynolds, 'Knowledge guardianship, custodianship and ethics'.

35 David Welchman Gegeo and Karen Ann Watson-Gegeo, '"How we know": Kwara'ae rural villagers doing indigenous epistemology', in *The Contemporary Pacific*, Vol. 13, Issue 1 (2001): 55-88.

36 Kabini Sanga, *Fānanau lā i Gula'alā* (Wellington: TNR Literatures, 2014).

37 Sanga and Reynolds, 'Knowledge guardianship, custodianship and ethics'.

38 John Iromea and Martyn Reynolds, 'Access, ethical leadership and action in Solomon Islands education: A *tok stori*', in *International Education Journal: Comparative Perspectives*, Vol. 20, Issue 3 (2021): 31-44.

39 Fito'o, 'Wantok-centred framework for developing citizenship'.

40 Paliaima Aiyery Tanda, 'An analytical evaluation of the effects of the *Wantok* System in the South Sea Evangelical Church of Papua New Guinea', in *Melanesian Journal of Theology*, in Vol. 27, Issue 1 (2011): 7-8.

41 Gideon Fangalea, 'An Analytical Evaluation of the Spirituality of the South Sea Evangelical church in the Solomon Islands', B.Th. thesis, CLTC, 2009, 15.

42 Tsutomu Kobayashi, Matthew Nicholson, Russell Hoye, 'Football "wantok": Sport and social capital in Vanuatu', in *International review for the Sociology of Sport*, Vol. 48, No. 1 (2013): 38-53.

43 A. A. Leana, *The positive impact of the Wantok System in Port Moresby: Evangelical Alliance Relationships*, Fuller Theological Seminary (Pasadina: School of Intercultural Studies, 2020).

44 Michael Otoara Ha'apio, Ricardo Gonzalez, Morgan Wairiu, 'Is there any chance for the poor to cope with extreme environmental events? Two case studies in the Solomon Islands', in *World Development*, Vol. 122 (October 2019): 514-524.

45 Tanda, 'An analytical evaluation of the effects of the *Wantok* System in the South Sea Evangelical Church of Papua New Guinea'; and Grant W. Walton, 'Establishing and maintaining the technical anti-corruption assemblage: the Solomon Islands experience', in *Third World Quarterly*, Vol. 41, No. 11 (2020): 1918-1936.

46 Fito'o, 'Wantok-centred framework for developing citizenship', 56.
47 Sanga and Martyn Reynolds, 'Melanesian *tok stori* in leadership development'.
48 Kabini Sanga, Jack Maebuta, Seu'ula Johansson-Fua, and Martyn Reynolds, 'Rethinking contextualisation in Solomon Islands school leadership professional learning and development, in *Pacific Dynamics*, Vol. 4, Issue 1 (2020): 17-29.

RESPONSES
Pasifika thought in modern Australia

An Australian in Honiara

Anouk Ride[*]

Dr Ride, you have a long association with Solomon Islands, including over a decade working as a social scientist in Honiara. How did your interest in Solomon Islands begin?

I lived a fairly nomadic life before coming to Solomon Islands, and I went there thinking I might be there a year or two in order to do my doctoral research. It wasn't something planned, but I did end up staying a long time, for family reasons and also for my own curiosity.

Solomon Islands is a fascinating place. It is a melting pot of Melanesian, Polynesian, and Micronesian peoples as well as being in the process of rapid changes from subsistence to cash economies, from old to modern technologies, from tribal ways and languages to more interactions with foreign migrants and the outside world and, increasingly, political and geopolitical changes.

In the international development sector in particular, staying in one place is often seen as a bad thing for your career. But in terms of being able to get stuff done, I've found the opposite: building relationships and layers of knowledge over time allows you to be a part of change.

---

[*] Anouk Ride is a social scientist for WorldFish. She holds a PhD from the University of Queensland and is affiliated to the University of Melbourne and Australian National University. She lives in Honiara, Solomon Islands.

Your PhD reframed the causes of conflicts in Solomon Islands by de-emphasising ethnicity and drawing attention to tensions between society and its elites. Has your thinking evolved on this question?

A few years after I finished the PhD conflict conditions worsened, there was unrest over the election of the current prime minister, the switch in bilateral relations from Taiwan to China, and relations and power-sharing (or lack of it) between provinces and the national government. All this unrest and these frictions have an underlying cause of disconnect between the elites in control of parliament and government and the people. So, if anything, my hypothesis that elite capture of the state is a fundamental cause of conflict has been proven right, but ethnic links are still important in how this cause manifests.

For example, leaders of, and dissenters from, the current government will try to rally supporters based on ethnic links. Psychology tells us people look through the lens of 'us' versus 'others', but researchers are not necessarily aware of ethnic stereotypes and lenses to the study of conflict in other countries. Researchers need to be more reflexive about their own biases and look for the evidence before presenting analyses that frame ethnicity as a cause of conflict. Some of the writing by academics outside Solomon Islands suggests that ethnicity divides Islanders, whereas there is far more peaceful coexistence and melding of ethnicities than conflict overall in its modern history.

Solomon Islands has made world news in recent years, including during the 2021 riots which you lived through and wrote about. In a 2020 article, you predicted that riots could soon break out from causes you could observe.

The 2021 riots were severe, caused widespread damage, a few deaths and were terrible for all who saw them. To add to that, I was disturbed because I thought the events were preventable and predictable and I had predicted a similar pattern of violence in an article

Synkrētic

for the Australian National University in December 2020.¹ It was sort of like seeing a nightmare you envisaged coming true, but at the time I was too tired and sad to write about it.

A friend called me and said, 'You *have* to write about this now, what has happened is exactly what you said would happen.' After that call, I wrote a piece for the Lowy Institute, which I hope was helpful in interpreting events.² We have to look beyond the day of the riot to understand how these processes happen, and what we can do to prevent them. Learning from history is our only hope for the future.

You have argued that writers outside Solomon Islands should not be too quick to reach for geopolitical explanations when analysing local events. Does this habit reflect a thin understanding of realities on the ground?

Up until recently, Solomon Islands was rarely in the news. Then it was the front page or leading story, and it was funny seeing all the commentators come up. I would estimate that around 90 per cent of the researchers interviewed were not in the country when events unfolded and had not been for some time, as Solomon Islands closed its borders for two years during COVID-19.

The political discourse was also extreme and did little to increase understanding of what was happening, something I and Initiative for Peacebuilding colleagues were very concerned about.³

So, few commentators had an idea of internal conditions and the geopolitical angle was an easy reach, simply assuming that local actors acted primarily because of geopolitical allegiances. However, people's motivations are complex, and this is certainly the case in Solomon Islands.

The prime minister might be "pro-China" but this is also linked to an idea of maintaining his centralised control of the country, a more authoritarian approach to governance and the like. Malaita province might be "pro-West" but this is positioning to try to maintain or strengthen their freedoms and abilities to govern their own affairs.

There is a fundamental power struggle within the country over inappropriate governance systems in need of reform, as Dr Transform Aqorau has pointed out.[4]

Structural change to governance needs to be addressed. That has nothing to do with geopolitics and everything to do with Solomon Islanders needing to decide what system of governance they want and can maintain themselves.

In 2021, the Australian Defence Force was invited by the government to help restore law and order, as it was during a period of civil conflict in 1998-2003. What is Australia's image among locals and does it affect your experience?

When I first went to Solomon Islands back in 2008 and started interacting with Solomon professionals and visiting communities, a comment I would get a lot is that I was different from other Australians. It took me a while to figure out what that meant, but I think there was this idea that Australians would come in and "run the show". They were known to have specific ideas about things, to be somewhat bossy, socialise largely among themselves, eat different foods, and behave differently and then leave.

Generally speaking, New Zealanders and Pacific Islanders who were part of the intervention known as the Regional Assistance Mission to Solomon Islands (RASMI) had a better image in the eyes of local people. This was a huge wake up call to me in terms of influencing how I behaved and seeing how other Australians behave in the Pacific more critically. I think Australians have this idea that they can walk into a room and be "mates" with anyone, but when you have history and huge power and cultural differentials between you and others, it's not that simple.

The Australians who worked well and were well liked were ones who listened, took their time, could work with different perspectives, and devolved power. This is particularly important now in relation to the security sector,[5] otherwise there is a danger at some point that Pacific countries will opt not to work with Australia on security matters.

Synkrētic

Australians' engagement with Solomon Islanders seems quite top-heavy in the sense of being driven by the government and development sector.

I am not sure I have much to say about this, except some colleagues have pointed to the need for more Australians to be more literate about the Pacific. And this is something I would support, but to be literate based on Pacific teachers and literature written by Pacific Islanders in order to break through our cultural biases and frames.

Do you think the bottom-up, that is social, cultural, religious, and private sector ties between Australians and Solomon Islanders are under-done?

One immediate concern I have at the moment is the increasing restrictions on freedom of speech and assembly in Solomon Islands. Several people in the NGO and religious sectors have been threatened by the police or by court cases, pursued by the government simply because of what they said in public or online forums.

I would hope to see more support by Australian civil society to Solomon Islands civil society, including local NGOs, the arts, youth and women's organisations and networks. Not just financial support but the support of friendship, exchange, prayer, even refuge if required. These ties can be powerful in more ways than one.

Synkrētic **has a strong interest in the oral forms of Pacific thought. Should the local concept of *tok stori* be seen as a method of philosophising?**

One of the exciting things about working in Solomon Islands at the moment is engaging with its leading scholars on indigenous methodologies, epistemologies and research. These discussions have always been around but are getting much more attention, and I would say even reshaping mainstream research in many fields.

I would love your readers to become more familiar with the work of Dr David Gegeo and Dr Kabini Sanga who are both leaders in this domain. They also have lectures and papers online as resources.

49

My friends and colleagues currently doing Masters and PhDs are mostly engaging with local research methods, sometimes in addition to other methods such as marine science, and I find this very exciting.

Tok stori is a method of philosophising but it is also a way of being, of relationships and relation not just to thoughts and concepts but to each other. This is one of the things that has been missing from mainstream science, to its detriment in my opinion. There is still much to be learnt across cultures, across methodologies, across the region.

What sources, writers, and thinkers could you recommend for readers wanting to explore Solomon Islanders' perspectives?

Some of those great academics I have mentioned: the writings of Dr Transform Aqorau, Dr Kabini Sanga, Dr David Gegeo and also Dr Alice Pollard and Dr Jack Maebuta. Also, the creative works of younger people, particularly film, such as Dreamcast Theatre productions, the films of the Lepping sisters, Chai Comedy and the works published by the Solomon Islands Creative Writers Association, which are mostly available at the University of the South Pacific. There is a lot of dynamism in the arts, women, and youth sectors and by tribal associations that reveal the thoughts and experiences of Solomon Islanders.

You have studied the sources of conflict. What are the sources of peace in Solomon Islands that give you and locals hope in the future?

Peace is about making peaceful choices at the individual, community, or national level. Australia can do what it can to ensure the next election is free and fair, to make sure its policing support is accountable and encourages accountability in the police force, and to learn more from past experiences of conflict, including its own role in shaping current conflict conditions.

Solomon Islanders have a number of ways to resolve the conflicts they have peacefully: through dialogue between people with

Synkrētic

different perspectives, through greater accountability of the state to the people, through decentralisation of governance, through increasing the transparency and accountability of the police force, and through community-led initiatives to prevent crime and conflict.

And as I said, women, youth, tribal and local leaders have the dynamism to keep pursuing peace and so they deserve support from Australian and Solomon leaders alike.

Notes

1. Anouk Ride, 'Solomon Islands' long summer of discontent: Security challenges', in *Development Bulletin*, eds. Pamela Thomas and Meg Keen, No. 82 (Feb. 2021): 156-158. Available at <https://crawford.anu.edu.au/rmap/devnet/devnet/DB82-final-manuscript-23-02-21.pdf>.
2. Anouk Ride, 'Honiara as the smoke subsides', *The Interpreter*, 26 November 2021, available at: <https://www.lowyinstitute.org/the-interpreter/honiara-smoke-subsides>.
3. Tania Miletic and Anouk Ride, 'Tensions are high between China and Australia over Solomon Islands, but it's in everyone's interests to simmer down', in *The Guardian*, 5 April 2022, available at: <https://www.theguardian.com/world/2022/apr/05/tensions-are-high-between-china-and-australia-over-solomon-islands-but-its-in-everyones-interests-to-simmer-down>.
4. Transform Aqorau and Anouk Ride, 'Solomon Islands: a blueprint to stop a cycle of strife', in *The Interpreter*, 29 August 2022, available at: <https://www.lowyinstitute.org/the-interpreter/solomon-islands-blueprint-stop-cycle-strife>.
5. Anouk Ride, 'New Australian Government Must Draw "Red Lines" In Solomon Islands', in *Australian Outlook*, 23 May 2022, available at: <https://www.internationalaffairs.org.au/australianoutlook/new-australian-government-must-draw-red-lines-in-solomon-islands/>.

Listening to Pasifika voices

*Jioji Ravulo**

Professor Ravulo, last year you became the first Pasifika professor in Australia. Was it a surprise to you that you were the first?

Very much so! I had no idea that this was the case until a Pasifika colleague, Pefi Kingi based in Victoria, posted about it on her social media platforms. I was genuinely surprised!

For me, it is a true honour and privilege to be noted as this. It is a shared achievement with and for our Pacific communities. However, many questions which prod and provoke my passions were raised. One question I had in particular was: 'Why? Why has it taken so long for universities in Australia to appoint a person from a Pasifika heritage as a professor?'

Traditionally, universities have been characterised as being very white and Westernised spaces that Pacific people may not be able to picture themselves in. We need to disrupt these perspectives and create opportunities to reshape the culture within to create environments and settings that are intentionally inclusive.

Everyone is involved in this conversation in which we can learn to embrace diverse perspectives and practices that support inclusive learning and teaching, and research and leadership.

---

* Jioji Ravulo is Professor and Chair of Social Work and Policy Studies in the Sydney School of Education and Social Work at The University of Sydney. He holds a PhD from Western Sydney University and lives in Sydney, Australia.

Synkrētic

Your research spans a broad range of social work issues, including the mental health of Pacific communities and NRL players of Pacific heritage. Was there a gap in the literature that led you to research Pasifika topics?

Yes, yes, and yes! The reason why I went into my doctorate was to help create empirical data on why there is an overrepresentation of Pasifika young people in the youth justice system. My social work career, before becoming an academic unintentionally, involved supporting young people who offend and their families, which included a large proportion of Pasifika in western Sydney. We didn't have any research on the reason why this may be occurring.

From this initial foray into research, I fell in love with the idea of being involved in supporting other Pacific-focussed research projects that would further assist our communities, whilst holding social systems and structures accountable for their interactions with us.

In essence, it's a shared solution where individuals, families, and communities help shape such service models of delivery and provision, rather than becoming vilified and victims to it. This includes health, education, legal, and welfare systems that can be designed to help diverse communities thrive.

At Western Sydney University, you have worked on programs to encourage students from a Pacific Island background to pursue tertiary study. Are they currently underrepresented in Australian universities, and if so why?

I started my first academic role as a Lecturer at Western Sydney University in July 2011 and was perplexed about why we didn't see may people from a Pacific heritage involved in this space. It led to the creation of Pasifika Achievement To Higher Education (PATHE), which celebrates its 10th anniversary in 2022.

In essence, the answer to our underrepresentation lies in the systems and structures that we implement within educational settings in Western societies. This includes the way we create and curate diverse learning styles and approaches that lead to meaningful educational engagement across all levels: early childhood, primary and high school, vocational and tertiary.

If we don't promote critical pedagogies and practices that enable diversity to be inclusive in teaching and learning, then we won't effectively support retention and progression towards further education and training. And this can mean ensuring Pacific epistemologies and ontologies are included in the scope of curricula, and that these harness our own narratives and lived experiences to support our educational involvement.

Through this approach, we can capture and enhance positive attitudes towards lifelong learning, which can further produce educational attainment towards social mobility and inclusion.

A news article noted that your father is Indigenous Fijian and moved to Australia in the 1970s where he met your mother.[1] How did being bicultural and the tensions of trying to negotiate two cultures shape your identity?

I was constantly challenged by the way in which other people were putting certain labels and binary perspectives on my identity.

This is captured (cheeky plug ahead) in a recent talk I did for TEDxSydney in August 2022 called 'Living beyond the binary'.[2] It is through my own lived experience of being biracial, bisexual, a person of colour and growing up in public housing in western Sydney that my ability to see the world beyond the binary was developed. In white, Western societies, we are obsessed with these binaries which create an us-and-them mentality and limit the opportunity to create safe spaces for everyone.

We need to move together towards a shared goal where our cultural diversity and its differences are seen as a source of celebration and help shape the communities in which we live.

Before becoming a professor, you trained as a singer and actor, and you still weave performance into your classes and participate in

comedy gigs in your spare time. Who were your artistic and intellectual influences growing up?

The performing arts continue to be of keen interest to me, and I've been fortunate enough to have had opportunities to be involved in various activities over the years. It's through these skills and attributes that I have been able to implement social work projects that support young people experiencing vulnerabilities to engage socially and therapeutically.

My artistic influences have been Pasifika people who have pioneered artistic spaces across the region. This includes Jay Laga'aia, who I first saw on the Australian TV show *Water Rats* back in the 1990s. He represented the possibility for people like us to be involved in these spaces.

Intellectually, Dr Epeli Hau'ofa has been a big influence through his insights, humour, and wit across poetry and stories that reflect our presence across Oceania. I'm also enthralled by the works of bell hooks, James Baldwin, and Paulo Freire.

You co-authored a 2022 article on the Sydney-based drill rap group ONEFOUR.[3] The Australian drill scene is notable for its many Polynesian rappers. What role does Pacific culture play in drillers like ONEFOUR?

The lyrics and sounds produced by groups like ONEFOUR are a reflection of our collectivist ideals and values as Pasifika people. Our identities are connected with community and reflect the spaces and places we traverse.

Certain themes may come across as being abrupt and challenging—but so they should. As a Pacific diaspora in Australia, we continue to be located in socioeconomic, socio-geographic, and socio-political contexts that reflect our marginality.

We should reflect on these narratives and see them as a source of knowledge that can be utilised to further support a shared understanding of our struggles, achievements, and all that is in between.

Additionally, ONEFOUR provides visibility to our existence within the Australian landscape, and moreso to our unique capabilities and strengths.

The article concludes that criminalising Pacific drillers counterproductively undermines important role models for their communities, who you note are over-represented in Australian prisons. Can music reverse that trend?

Music is part of the solution. In my own work with young offenders, we ran music projects to assist in their ability to share their lived experiences through song.

As Pasifika people, music has been used as a form of oratory and the passing down of our stories over generations. By learning from these experiences, we can create solutions that support the meeting of certain social and welfare needs that contribute to criminogenic factors that lead to offending.

At the same time, we need to decolonise the punitive nature of carceral spaces and reinvest in resources that support our communities. Failure to do this will continue to perpetuate our overrepresentation, leading to ongoing deficits and the dehumanisation of our peoples.

Australia's diplomatic, economic, and social ties to the Pacific have been receiving more mainstream media attention in recent years. While long part of the Pacific region, is Australia's sensitivity to its cultures improving?

I would like to think so. However, if we continue to operate within a context of paternalism, in which we view our interactions as being in the vested interests of the Pacific nations, then we continue to perpetuate neo-colonial and neo-imperial ways.

As the world is driven by its obsession for neoliberal leanings that enable consumerism and individualism to run rampant, Indigenous Pacific worldviews are further diminished and demoralised.

Synkrētic

If Australia wants to play a leading role in the region, then it needs to learn to understand our cultural views and values, and how this can shape collaborative cooperation across Oceania.

This can include consulting with the growing Pasifika diaspora in Australia, who continue to interact with and support families in our Islands of origin. We can help shape foreign policy in the Pacific and support the economic and social development of our countries of origin.

At a time of national soul-searching on the recognition of Indigenous Australians' identities, do you hear the voices of Pasifika, South Sea Islander and other Pacific communities also getting stronger in Australian society?

I believe our voice continues to evolve. I'm keen to ensure our ability to be involved across different sections of society is part of this picture, and that our perspectives and practices pervade the workplace resulting in culturally nuanced and safe spaces. We are greatly capable of being across all workforce sectors and industries, which will result in our ability to be represented.

However, for this to occur we need to create a shared approach to enshrining First Nations Australians as being key to everyone's success. We need to ensure that our culture as a country is constructed from a foundation that esteems Indigenous Australian voices, a treaty, and their truths. From this, I believe other ethnically diverse communities can be valued for their differences and help shape a national narrative driven by this context.

The 'West is best', 'white is right' discourse continues to be of disservice and creates disunity. We can learn so much from each other, if we learn to just get over ourselves individually, and practice collectivist view and values that are embedded within Indigenous paradigms.

As the first, what issue do you hope the fifth Pasifika professor in Australia will find resolved in their day that is still a challenge for you in your own?

At the time of writing, there are now three Pasifika professors in Australia— Professor Katerina Teaiwa, Professor Tu'uhevaha Kaitu'u-Lino, and me—so I'm confident the fourth and fifth are not too far off!

I would love to see a region where Indigenous Pacific people are at the table where conversations are being had about them as a people. Too often, we as Pacific people are being told what to do based on other people's decisions and determinations for us as population.

I envision an Oceania that promotes Pacific autonomy, determination, and agency that is not negatively impacted by the need to perceivably keep up with the West.

I know this sounds grandiose. However, if we could incorporate our Pacific perspectives within our modern social structures, systems, and settings, we would have much better health, educational, legal, and welfare outcomes. It's achievable, and we need to work together to create policy across all realms that can make this difference.

And having Pasifika professors in Australia is one part of this shared approach and solution.

Notes

1 Jordan Baker, '"It's been a journey": Meet Australia's first Pasifika professor', *Sydney Morning Herald*, available at: <https://www.smh.com.au/national/it-s-been-a-journey-meet-australia-s-first-pasifika-professor-20210329-p57evh.html>.

2 Jioji Ravulo, 'Living beyond the binary: decolonising Queer communities', *TEDxSydney*, 31 August 2022, available at: <https://www.youtube.com/watch?v=-nUXX-Td8EA>.

3 Murray Lee, Toby Martin, Jioji Ravulo, Ricky Simandjuntak, '[Dr]illing in the name of: the criminalisation of Sydney drill group ONEFOUR', in *Current Issues in Criminal Justice*, 8 August 2022, DOI: <https://doi.org/10.1080/10345329.2022.2100131>.

The ripple effect of blackbirding

*Amie Batalibasi**

Between 1864 and 1904, an estimated 60,000 Pacific islanders were abducted, deceived, and forced into working in Queensland's sugar plantations and in cotton farming. As an Australian Solomon Islander, is this history personal?

This history still very much remains under-acknowledged, yet it is a history that has had a ripple effect throughout the Pacific, Australia, and the world.

My heritage lies in the Solomon Islands, specifically Malaita Province. Estimates state that around 10,000 islanders came to Australia from that region alone. This had an impact of not only depopulating the islands, it also contributed to a severe loss of family, connection, and culture. Others were taken to island nations such as Fiji.

Most definitely this history is personal, especially because I have ancestors who were blackbirded and never seen or heard from again.

You produce Australian South Sea Islander Stories, a repository of family histories, photos, and sources on the legacy of "blackbird-

---

* Amie Batalibasi is an Australian-Solomon Islander filmmaker and founder of Colour Box Studio. She holds a Master of Film and TV from Melbourne University VCA and lives on the lands of the Kulin Nation, Melbourne, Australia.

ing", *i.e.* the enslavement of Pacific islanders in Australia. How did this project begin?

Australian South Sea Islander (ASSI) Stories started as a one-off project funded through the Australia Council for the Arts in 2014. I was the creative producer working in collaboration with the Australian South Sea Islanders Secretariat Inc. in Brisbane.

Throughout the year-long project, ASSI community members participated in filmmaking workshops and were supported to write, direct, and edit their own short films to present at a public screening. It was such a nourishing process of sharing, laughing, and learning together along the way. When the project ended, I voluntarily kept the website and socials[1] running because the response online has been amazing.[2]

Every August, I share archival materials, official documents, articles, ship records, name search indexes, videos, and photographs as part of the ASSI Stories project initiative, ASSI History Month. A lot of the information is in the public domain already, but the idea is to make it more accessible to our communities. People from around Australia and the Pacific follow along, comment, and connect.

Sharing these histories is a reclamation of these stories, connecting them back to the community when they have previously been held by institutions for decades or in some instances over 100 years. It's an attempt to shed some light on a dark part of our collective history.

You have also been involved with Pacific Community Partnerships Inc. (PCP), an association set up to connect Pacific Islander communities and which has facilitated projects in Solomon Islands. What does PCP do?

Initially we set up PCP with a small group of friends to embark on community projects in my village. Since 2009, we've supported projects around small gardens, disaster management, health and nutrition training, water tanks, sanitation projects as well as solar power training.

Synkrētic

We're now a registered incorporated association and this year, when the Covid-19 pandemic hit the Solomons really hard, we were able to fundraise for some emergency food and medical supplies to help those in need. We work with local groups in the village to make sure the projects are community-driven.

At the moment, we're developing projects to address the rising high tides and issues caused by the effects of climate change.

In 2010, you released *Tide of Change*. Filmed in Malaita, Solomon Islands, it is a documentary about climate change on this island. Climate change has become such a central issue in the Pacific. What inspired you to film this?

I made *Tide of Change* when I went back to my village to visit my *Koko Geli* (grandmother) who was very ill. It was a time when the high tides were ever-present, literally lapping at our feet.

After her passing and through our mourning, I was compelled to film what was happening in my village. It became a personal documentation of my family but also showed the effects of climate change.

Since then, the film has travelled around the world and I'm so grateful that we were able to connect with audiences and encourage dialogue around climate change in the Pacific.

You directed the award-winning *Blackbird* (2015), which was screened in 40 regional countries and at 17 festivals such as the 69th Berlinale International Film Festival. How has this moving film shaped discussion of blackbirding?

There are so many wonderful ASSI community members and organisations who have put in the hard yards to fight for recognition and respect here in Australia. I feel honoured to have had the opportunity to collaborate with various ASSI and Pacific Islander communities as well as my own family in order to acknowledge the history of blackbirding through community projects.

The impact of *Blackbird* is difficult to measure. But I can say that for a short film of 13 minutes made 7 years ago, the film continues

The ripple effect of blackbirding

to screen around the world. Our next festival screening is in Greece this year. When I've been present at screenings, people come up to me and say: 'I didn't know.'

When I took the film back to the village people asked to watch it over and over again. There is a curiosity around this subject matter and there is a hunger from the community to see themselves represented on screen.

I think that *Blackbird* is one story in a sea of so many to be told. Moving forward it's important that we, the community, are given the opportunity to tell the story from our own perspectives because for so long the narrative has been held by others.

In 2017, you co-directed *Ka Puta, Ko Au* with fellow Indigenous filmmakers Renae Maihi and Kelton Stepanowich for the Māoriland Film Festival. What was it like to work on this film set in pre-colonial Aotearoa New Zealand?

We made *Ka Puta, Ko Au* as part of a 72-hour film challenge for the festival. So, we wrote the story, had consultations, filmed, and edited the whole thing extremely fast. It definitely was a challenge but for me it was an honour to be working with Renae, Kelton, and the team.

The timing was just after I had received the Sundance Merata Mita Fellowship for that year. Merata Mita was the first Indigenous woman to solo direct a feature film in New Zealand, so it was so special to be there on the ground in Aotearoa because she clearly left a legacy, one that has impacted me as well.

***Synkrētic* features the stories and philosophies of Pacific cultures, which often take the form of oral history. Can readers access resources on the oral history that South Sea islanders brought to Australia in the 19th century?**

In my experience, oral histories have been accessed through my own curiosity sitting with my elders, drinking *bora* (tea) in the islands. Through my project work in Australia, I've been honoured to be included in conversations that are safe spaces to share.

Synkrētic

In terms of the archives, if you dig deep our stories are there between the lines and behind the black and white images. The research process can be quite an emotional journey, particularly when this history is embedded in racist government policies. But it can also be enlightening at times because, truly, knowledge is power.

I created a Resource page on the ASSI Stories website and when people contact me wanting to search for ancestors that's where I send them.[3]

How do Australian South Sea Islander stories continue to inspire your work?

I'm constantly inspired by our Australian South Sea Islander and Pacific Islander communities. Our stories, past and present, empower us. They demonstrate our resilience. That's what keeps me going.

Notes

1. Australian South Sea Islander Stories (ASSI), available at: <https://assistories.org/>. Instagram, Facebook, and Twitter accounts available at the handle: <@assistories>.
2. See also Amie Batalibasi's website: <https://amiebatalibasi.com/>.
3. 'Resources', ASSI, available at: <https://assistories.org/resources/>.

On Pacific logic

James D. Sellmann*

Professor Sellmann, you are Professor of Philosophy and Micronesian Studies at the University of Guam. How do both of these fascinating fields intersect, and do you teach Micronesian philosophy in your dual-hatted role?

I studied Euro-American, Asian, and Comparative philosophy at the University of Hawaii. In 1992, when I was hired at the University of Guam, the contract asked me to bring CHamoru studies into my discipline. So, I developed a course on CHamoru philosophy. Then I expanded the scope of my research to include other Micronesian cultural philosophies. I developed and taught a graduate course on Micronesian Philosophy.

My motivation is to bring the cultural philosophies of Micronesia and the greater Pacific into the academy for further study and benefit for all people. I also wanted to delve into the roots of Pacific philosophy by examining the logic, the ways of reasoning, which inform islander cultures and thinking.

At *Synkrētic*, we're focussed on the cultural philosophies of the Pacific and are sensitive to the oral forms they often take. Is it fair to say that Western academic philosophy struggles to see it as on par with Kant and Hume?

---

*   James D. Sellmann is Dean and Professor of Philosophy and Micronesian Studies, University of Guam. He holds a PhD in Chinese philosophy from the University of Hawaii and lives in Talofofo, Guam.

Synkrētic

In our global context, I think "we" ought to get beyond the East/West distinction because it is based on a Euro-centric colonial perspective, and from our Pacific perspective the cultures referred to are in the opposite direction. One of the reasons why institutionalised, academic philosophers are leery of cultural philosophy from an oral tradition is twofold.

First, because oral philosophy is not written down, it is difficult to ascertain its content.

Second, it is difficult if not impossible to see or read the development of that oral tradition's "grand conversation", also known as the historical changes of the tradition. Part of my motivation is to bring Pacific Philosophy into the academy to record its history.

I am aware that there are cultural experts who disagree and prefer to preserve the oral teachings without recording them to maintain the fluid character of the teachings, allowing the impermanent past to disappear by integrating into the present.

In 2021, you published a thought-provoking paper in Pacific Asia Inquiry on Micronesian philosophy and 'correlative thinking' which you distinguish from scientific logic.[1] What are the defining traits of this type of thought?

One characteristic of correlative thinking is to avoid stipulative definitions. Definitions give the impression that the defined object is locked into a category, especially the classical, scientific approach of definition by genus and species. I'd propose that correlative thinking looks to identify family resemblances.

Modern logic is based on the three principles of identity (A=A); the excluded middle (A is true or A is not true); and non-contradiction (not both A and not A).

Those three principles do not exactly apply in correlative thinking.

Correlative thinking acknowledges a dynamic process ontology, embracing change. The change is radical such that things transform, obscuring their identity. Inanimate objects are simultaneously gods. Certain Gods are humans, and certain humans are gods.

Rather than an excluded middle, an inclusive middle is emphasised such that the changing nature of things allows them to be and not to be at the same time. The interrelated character of the correlated opposites leaves one's thinking open to a more complex arrangement of "both A and not A and something else". Relationality and relationships are more important in correlative thinking than independent substances.

In correlative thinking there is room for not only inconsistencies but even direct contradictions to be accepted. This kind of thinking leaves open the possibilities for changing truths and knowledge; it is not based on the pursuit of absolute, precise, unchanging knowledge claims.

Modern logicians would label correlative thinking as fuzzy logic.

You write that ancient Micronesians did not develop monistic or dualistic philosophies as in Western tradition, e.g. theories that the world is made up of one or two substances like body and spirit. Is this true across the Pacific?

I know that I do not know the correct answer to this question because the Pacific covers more than one-third of the surface of the globe. I have not been able to study all the cultures of the Pacific and their histories. Given the unknown past of Pacific oral teaching, it could be possible that there were ancient monists or dualists in the Pacific.

Part of the claim that ancient peoples used correlative thinking is grounded in brain science (see the paper's Appendix IV, 'The Correlative Character of Human Cognition'). The idea is that correlative thinking dominated ancient human cognition globally. Over time, correlative thinking was replaced by other forms of cognition.

As the ancient cultural philosophies in South, Southeast and East Asia continued to change over time, creating monistic and dualistic philosophies, they too entered the Pacific. First Hindu and Buddhist philosophies entered the Pacific, and later Islamic and Christian philosophies came, bringing in monism and dualism.

Synkrētic

Pacific islanders seem to reject a principle of logic established by Aristotle: that a claim must either be right or wrong, never both. You say that Pacific islanders think in terms of true-and-false. Could you provide an example?

Last week the university launched our Certificate in Traditional Navigation program. Part of the ceremony was the enactment of the *Pow* (to pound) ritual to initiate new navigators. A palm frond is used to symbolically beat arrogance out of the initiate while pounding in humility. In the process, the initiates become possessed by ancestral spirits.

Traditionally, the initiates would go into isolation for four days and be given a different herbal medicine each day until they may return to community life. The initiates are both bodily-humans and spiritual-ancestors at the same time. There are many stories across the Pacific of gods and goddesses presenting as humans or inanimate objects. They are both true spirits and not true spirits, but physical at the same time.

In Belau, a drunk driver killed a pedestrian. The Justice Department wanted to put him on trial for, clearly, he was guilty. The victim's family wanted to adopt him to replace their son. He was truly guilty and truly not guilty as the adopted son. When everything is understood to be interconnected, hard and fast categories melt and blend.

In the Pacific and in other regions, ancestors do not leave but live on after death in the same world as us in a nearby village, valley, or cave. Hell and heaven are on earth, not another realm. This is an ancient concept, isn't it?

I agree. Globally, across ancient cultures the deceased ancestors were still nearby. They could continue to assist or punish their relatives. The idea that the dearly departed reside in transcendent realms, such as heaven, purgatory, or hell, far beyond and very different from the physical world is based on a dualism that separates the material world from an abstract pure spiritual realm.

On Pacific logic

As you point out, in many Pacific cultures like the Chuukese of Micronesia and CHamorus of Guam, gods become people and vice versa. Does this remind you of ancient European traditions, for example Greek myths?

If the brain science is correct that human cognition is correlative in character, then it is not surprising to find ancient cross-cultural universals. The god becoming human, the personal relationship with the saviour, and the human blood sacrifice motif are some of the elements that make Christianity so popular and easy for folks to convert to.

You write that many moderns identify with abstract belief systems, *i.e.* with a religious, political, or scientific worldview, while Pacific traditions identify with their ancestors. How do Pacific islanders strive to balance both worlds?

That is a complex question. The practice is not to balance two different things or approaches but to integrate them in a "both and something more" perspective. In politics, some Pacific nations' constitutions give cultural-political capital to village leaders or chiefs. Extended families form political parties and vote accordingly. In the church or temple, we express our hopes, values, and beliefs in our own cultural modes.

The human brain learns by making mistakes and by drawing analogies from past experiences. Drawing analogies is part of correlative thinking. In practice, scientific approaches were always part of island wisdom. Islanders have always quickly adopted and integrated technology into our lives. The modern Pacific scientific laboratories contain island wisdom.

You conclude that non-Pacific islanders too need not choose between the monist and dualist philosophies that underlie modern technology. What can Westerners learn from Pacific philosophies?

Some of the topics that modern peoples across the continents can learn from Pacific philosophies are the importance of relationality and relationship in both the social and natural realms.

Synkrētic

The climate crisis is in part due to a lack of understanding and appreciation for how human actions and consumption effect the environment. The heart of Pacific philosophy is the beat and rhythm of the environment. Pacific philosophies are first and foremost environmental philosophies.

The rest of the world needs to tune into indigenous ecological thinking because the dualistic model of humans dominating a wild nature is not working well. Human society is part and parcel of the environment. Social and political harmony are rooted in environmental resources.

The onto-cosmic relationality between all life, including human life and the environment, is sacred. As such, human relationships are also sacred. The fragmentation of modern social life would be better informed by the importance of maintaining relationships.

Ancient Hindu creation stories, you explain, travelled the world as far as Ireland and turn up in Pacific stories. As a student of both Chinese and Pacific philosophy, do you see much overlap between these traditions?

The strongest similarity is the use of correlative thinking. Early 20th century Sinologists mistakenly claimed that yin-yang (correlative) thinking was unique to China. A.C. Graham first exposed the universal nature of correlative thinking. W. Goodenough noted the numerology connection between the Chinese Yijing 易經 (*Book of Changes*) and Chuuk divination practices. So, we can say there was some direct transmission from the China mainland into the Pacific beyond Taiwan and Japan.

Thank you for this opportunity to dialogue with you.

Notes

1   James D. Sellmann, 'Correlative Thinking in Pacific Island (Micronesian) Cultural Philosophies', in *Pacific Asia Inquiry, Multidisciplinary Perspectives*, Vol. 11, No. 1 (Fall 2020): 153-175.

STORIES

He

*Dorell Ben**

The water danced and glistened like sapphire jewels. The sun's powerful beams drew sweat, and its warmth swaddled him. He could taste the salt in the air and hear the wind through the trees and bushes behind him that carried the sweet scent of flowers.

He would always remember his Rotuma this way. Crystal clear ocean all around, shades of blues, sweltering breezes of fragrant salt, and the soft waves rhythmically beating the white, sandy beaches. He sighed as though a weight pulled him inwards, picked up a small rock and tossed it at the waves, somehow hoping the rock would take his worries into the sea with it. He watched the waves reclaim the small rock, wash up to touch the fishing net lying on the beach, and return to the same ocean. He sighed again. A fear was brewing in his chest, where an aching pain gripped him.

He knew today would be the day he'd tell his father, the day he'd soon leave his island. He knew he'd miss it and its people. He would miss home.

On his walk back home, he forced himself to cheer up. The walk through the coconut tree plantations was meditative. The tall trees reached for the skies, the grass all around his feet sprouted like the land's caring spirits. His little home was not too far from the beach.

---

* Dorell Ben is a Gujarati-Rotuman woman from Fiji. She is currently studying for a PhD in the reawakening of Indigenous Oceanic women's cultural tattoo practices at Griffith University.

He

At night, he would sometimes stay awake just to listen to the waves purr a lullaby.

As he approached home, he could smell his mother's cooking and the smoke of his father's cigarette. He saw his father sitting at a table, staring out of the open door. He greeted his two younger brothers and put a flower in his mother's ear. He glanced at his father. The man took the shirt hanging over his shoulder and swatted at the flies. He flinched at the sound of it hitting the table, reminding him of the temper that slept within his father.

'Where you been, ay? Daydreaming again? You lazy!' his father said.

'I went to the beach,' he said and hung his head respectfully low.

'Ha! To fish? You lazy bum. You don't know how to fish.'

'Leave him alone,' his mother said, gesturing for him to stir the pot. It was a temporary reprieve from his father's cutting words.

'Your aunty is coming by the boat today. You should go help her bring some things home.'

'I want to go!' his little brother piped up.

'No! You have to stay here and help me cook the food,' his mother said. She was a very softly spoken woman and was full of all sorts of stories. Today, she chose to talk about Kirkirsasa and the Giant. The legend of Kirkirsasa came up because of the *tāhroro*[1] she was preparing for dinner that night.

The story went that, one day, a woman named Kirkirsasa sent two girls to the sea to fetch seawater. Taking their time with the chore, the girls came across a sleeping giant. They began to throw rocks at the giant, whose angry eyes cracked open and who, in a rage, chased them back to Kirkirsasa's home.

His mother lunged for the boys on the floor, imitating the giant chasing the girls. Laughter and shrill little screams of excitement erupted from the boys.

'Ay!' came his father's shriek that filled their house with fearful silence. 'Shut up!'

He exchanged knowing glances with his mother. She gently stroked his back, then continued the story with a hushed tone while she served the food.

Synkrētic

To appease the giant, Kirkirsasa began to dance and sing for him. She revealed her tattooed armpits and slapped them, which calmed the giant's rage. After her dance, Kirkirsasa and the giant made a bargain. She would tattoo his armpits for him, and in exchange he would not eat the two girls. Kirkirsasa got everyone in the village to build a great, big fire and heat stones on it until they glowed red. But in an act of trickery, Kirkirsasa and her people placed the hot stones onto him instead, killing the giant and saving the two girls.

He could never understand why Kirkirsasa had tattooed her arm pits. Perhaps Kirkirsasa's story was about what happened to people who did not do as they were told. Or maybe it was about how graceful her dance was to appease the giant.

He looked at his father with the giant still on his mind. The old man slapped his thigh like always and lowered himself to the mat to eat. They were sitting in a circle but no one touched their food. The man took in a long sniff, then coughed wetly. Phlegm was stuck in his throat, which his sputtering couldn't dislodge completely.

'In the name of the Father, and of the Son, and of the Holy Spirit,' he said praying in Rotuman. It was a very long prayer, thanking God for everything and asking God for more. 'Amen,' they all said in unison, opening their eyes at the end.

He will miss his mother's *tähroro*. It had a very distinct taste. And whenever he'd asked her what she did to make it taste different, she'd said the same cryptic thing. 'Love. Just add a bit of love,' she'd said ruffling his hair.

'What are you smiling about,' his father said. 'Tomorrow, you going to your *ma'piga* to cut her grass. Do some work, eh, you lazy bum.'

He felt a heavy hand hit the back of his head.

'You listening? Or you daydreaming again?' his father said.

'I won't be coming home.'

His words felt like a flame wavering in a heavy storm.

'What did you say?' his father said, holding his fork in mid-air just outside his gaping mouth.

He felt his field of vision shrink. His clammy skin was burning up. Was his father really the giant? Would he have to sing and dance for this giant? A new feeling took hold of him. It was not fear. Perhaps, now, the stones were hot enough for him to scorch his giant.

'I said…' he began with a shaky voice, taking a deep breath to continue, '…I won't be…'

He did not get to finish his sentence. The giant's hand came down hard on his face. It sent him sprawling on the mat. He could smell the frond leaves woven into it. His ears rang, muffling the sounds of his mother attempting to soothe his father. He saw his own blood and sweat mix together on a weave, forming a cloud. His hearing slowly returned. He took in another deep breath and, getting up, found his voice to yell back at his father.

'I'm going to *Fiti*!³ Then I'm going overseas!'

'With what money, huh? You lazy all the time. Who will pay the ticket to *Fiti*? You stealing from me!'

His father stood up and kicked him without warning. His legs slid back as he took the blow and coughed up blood. Still standing, he faced his father.

'My boyfriend gave me the money.'

He saw the twitch in the giant's confused eyes. The room grew so quiet that he could hear his shallow heartbeat thumping in his ear. Then his mother's soft singing broke the silence. She sang Kirkirsasa's song to soothe her two younger boys. And to placate the giant. He hugged his mother, breathed her in. He kissed his two brothers, grabbed his bag, and left quietly.

He could hear his father's voice fading behind him with each step.

'Don't come back here!'

'You're a disgrace!'

'You will suffer in hell!'

'You lazy bum!'

He paused to feel the sand between his toes, and left the giant and his family.

His smiling boyfriend was waiting for him when he disembarked from the boat. They had spoken many times about him leaving his father, in so many letters exchanged over the years. And when he was finally ready to start his new life, his boyfriend was there to help him do it. The first thing he was going to do was to be brave and get himself a tattoo. He had thought about it on the journey over to Fiji. He was adamant about getting one before leaving for overseas.

'Why a tattoo? I didn't know you were that sort of a bad boy,' his boyfriend said chuckling and draped an arm around him. 'I have a friend who can help you.'

Over several days he sat on a chair, listening to the buzzing sound of the tattoo machine. He absorbed the pain differently, noticing how it didn't hurt as much as when his father struck and kicked him. When the tattoo was completed and the swelling had begun to subside, he went home to his boyfriend and a small gathering of unfamiliar faces, all beaming back at him. In the weeks that followed, when the swelling had begun to subside, he had come home one evening to his boyfriend and a small gathering of unfamiliar faces, all beaming at him.

'Who are these people?' he asked.

His boyfriend squeezed his hand reassuringly.

'I learned that you needed a *hapagsū*[4] performed after the tattoo. So, I had a few friends help.'

He hadn't had one done for himself. But he remembered being part of a larger ceremony back home. A man would say some words in Rotuman, and people would respond to appease the spirits. His uncle had an operation and needed a *hapagsū* performed. His uncle passed when he was a little boy. And now here he was, getting one for himself. He was not sure if performing one was required for him. He was not sure if his father's curse would affect him during one and if he would eventually end up like his uncle. After all the formalities, they had a feast and danced. Then, when it was just the two of them, he felt all his worries disappear.

'Can I see it now?' His boyfriend grinned at him.

He nodded. 'I want to see it too.'

They stepped into the bedroom, and he stood in front of the mirror, shaking. He took his shirt off and saw the marks protruding just above the waistband of his trousers. He felt his boyfriend touch the middle of his back as he unbuttoned his trousers and pulled them off.

'Whoa!'

He faced his boyfriend.

'What? What do you think?'

'It looks amazing! He tattooed you really well. One day you have to tell me what these mean. Can I touch it?'

He turned to face the mirror and looked at himself. He could see the ocean waves rising, the trees around his home, the fishing net he left at the beach, and the flowers that were once in his mother's hair.

'They are me. These represent me and my *hanua*.'[5]

His boyfriend hugged him.

'We will reconnect you with your family, my love. One day.'

He felt so much freedom and happiness. They embraced and he knew that, no matter how far he would go now, he would always have these memories with him.

Notes

1 *Tähroro*: fermented coconut condiment.
2 *ma'piga*: grandparent.
3 *Fiti*: Fiji.
4 *Hapagsü*: feast given to / for a person after an operation or illness.
5 *Hanua*: home or land.

The jumping stones*

Bronisław Malinowski[†]

Let us return now to our Sinaketan fleet, moving southwards along the barrier reef and sighting one small island after the other. If they did not start very early from Muwa—and delay is one of the characteristics of native life—and if they were not favoured with a very good wind, they would probably have to put in at one of the small sand islands, Legumatabu, Gabuwana or Yakum. Here, on the western side, sheltered from the prevalent trade winds, there is a diminutive lagoon, bounded by two natural breakwaters of coral reef running from the Northern and Southern ends of the island. Fires are lit on the clean, white sand, under the scraggy pandanus trees, and the natives boil their yam food and the eggs of the wild sea fowl, collected on the spot. When darkness closes in and the fires draw them all into a circle, the Kula talk begins again.

Let us listen to some such conversations, and try to steep ourselves in the atmosphere surrounding this handful of natives, cast for a while on to the narrow sandbank, far away from their

---

* This story is based on the accounts of unnamed informants from Papua New Guinea's Trobriand people. Edited extract from Bronisław Malinowski, *Argonauts of the Western Pacific: An Account of Native Enterprise and Adventure in the Archipelagoes of Melanesian New Guinea* (London: Routledge & Kegan Paul Ltd., 1966 [1922]), 232-235. This work is in the public domain.

† Bronisław Malinowski was a prominent Polish-British anthropologist. He held a PhD in philosophy, mathematics, and physics from Jagiellonian University and lived in Kraków, London, and New Haven.

79

The jumping stones

homes, having to trust only to their frail canoes on the long journey which faces them. Darkness, the roar of surf breaking on the reef, the dry rattle of the pandanus leaves in the wind, all produce a frame of mind in which it is easy to believe in the dangers of witches and all the beings usually hidden away, but ready to creep out at some special moment of horror. The change of tone is unmistakable, when you get the natives to talk about these things on such an occasion, from the calm, often rationalistic way of treating them in broad daylight in an ethnographer's tent. Some of the most striking revelations I have received of this side of native belief and psychology were made to me on similar occasions. Sitting on a lonely beach in Sanaroa, surrounded by a crew of Trobrianders, Dobuans, and a few local natives, I first heard the story of the jumping stones. On a previous night, trying to anchor off Gumasila in the Amphletts, we had been caught by a violent squall, which tore one of our sails, and forced us to run before the wind, on a dark night, in the pouring rain. Except for myself, all the members of the crew saw clearly the flying witches in the form of a flame at the mast head. Whether this was St. Elmo's fire I could not judge, as I was in the cabin, seasick and indifferent to dangers, witches, and even ethnographic revelations. Inspired by this incident, my crew told me how this is, as a rule, a sign of disaster, how such a light appeared a few years ago in a boat, which was sunk almost on the same spot where the squall had caught us; but fortunately all were saved. Starting from this, all sorts of dangers were spoken about, in a tone of deep conviction, rendered perfectly sincere by the experiences of the previous night, the surrounding darkness, and the difficulties of the situation—for we had to repair our sail and again attempt the difficult landing in the Amphletts.

I have always found that whenever natives are found under similar circumstances, surrounded by the darkness and the imminent possibility of danger, they naturally drift into a conversation about the various things and beings into which the fears and apprehensions of generations have traditionally crystallised.

Thus, if we imagine that we listen to an account of the perils and horrors of the seas, sitting round the fire at Yakum or Legumatabu,

Synkrētic

we do not stray from reality. One of those who are specially versed in tradition, and who love to tell a story, might refer to one of his own experiences; or to a well-known case from the past, while others would chime in, and comment, telling their own stories. General statements of belief would be given, while the younger men would listen to the tales so familiar, but always heard with renewed interest.

They would hear about an enormous octopus (*kwita*) which lies in wait for canoes, sailing over the open seas. It is not an ordinary *kwita* of exceptional size, but a special one, so gigantic that it would cover a whole village with its body; its arms are thick as coconut palms, stretching right across the sea. With typical exaggeration, the natives will say: '*ikanubwadi Pilolu,*'... 'he covers up all the Pilolu' (the sea-arm between the Trobriands and the Amphletts). Its proper home is in the East, '*o Muyuwa,*' as the natives describe that region of sea and islands, where also it is believed some magic is known against the dreadful creature. Only seldom does it come to the waters between the Trobriands and Amphletts, but there are people who have seen it there. One of the old men of Sinaketa tells how, coming from Dobu, when he was quite young, he sailed in a canoe ahead of the fleet, some canoes being to the right and some to the left behind him. Suddenly from his canoe, they saw the giant *kwita* right in front of them. Paralysed with fear, they fell silent, and the man himself, getting up on the platform, by signs warned the other canoes of the danger. At once they turned round, and the fleet divided into two, took big bends in their course, and thus gave the octopus a wide berth. For woe to the canoe caught by the giant *kwita*! It would be held fast, unable to move for days, till the crew, dying of hunger and thirst, would decide to sacrifice one of the small boys of their number. Adorned with valuables, he would be thrown overboard, and then the *kwita*, satisfied, would let go its hold of the canoe, and set it free. Once a native, asked why a grown-up would not be sacrificed on such an occasion, gave me the answer:

> A grown-up man would not like it; a boy has got no mind. We take him by force and throw him to the *kwita*.

The jumping stones

Another danger threatening a canoe on the high seas is a big, special rain, or water falling from above, called *Sinamatanoginogi*. When in rain and bad weather a canoe, in spite of all the efforts to bail it out, fills with water, *Sinamatanoginogi* strikes it from above and breaks it up. Whether at the basis of this are the accidents with waterspouts, or cloudbursts or simply extremely big waves breaking up the canoe, it is difficult to judge. On the whole, this belief is more easily accounted for than the previous one.

The most remarkable of these beliefs is that there are big, live stones, which lie in wait for sailing canoes, run after them, jump up and smash them to pieces. Whenever the natives have reasons to be afraid of them, all the members of the crew will keep silence, as laughter and loud talk attracts them. Sometimes they can be seen, at a distance, jumping out of the sea or moving on the water. In fact, I have had them pointed to me, sailing off Koyatabu, and although I could see nothing, the natives, obviously, genuinely believed they saw them. Of one thing I am certain, however, that there was no reef awash there for miles around. The natives also know quite well that they are different from any reefs or shallows, for the live stones move, and when they perceive a canoe will pursue it, break it up on purpose and smash the men. Nor would these expert fishermen ever confuse a jumping fish with anything else, though in speaking of the stones they may compare them to a leaping dolphin or stingray.

There are two names given to such stones. One of them, *nuwakekepaki*, applies to the stones met in the Dobuan seas. The other, *vineylida*, to those who live '*o Muyuwa.*' Thus, in the open seas, the two spheres of culture meet, for the stones not only differ in name but also in nature. The *nuwakekepaki* are probably nothing but malevolent stones. The *vineylida* are inhabited by witches, or according to others, by evil male beings. Sometimes a *vineylida* will spring to the surface, and hold fast the canoe, very much in the same manner as the giant octopus would do. And here again offerings would have to be given. A folded mat would first be thrown, in an attempt to deceive it; if this were of no avail, a little boy would be anointed with coconut oil, adorned with arm-shells and *bagi* necklaces, and thrown over to the evil stones.

The first people*

Claire Moyse-Faurie,[†] *Corneille Nonké,*
Philibert Nékaré, Marinette Oundo,
Marceline Até, Maria Thavivianon

TRANSLATED BY *Daryl Morini*[‡]

I
Corneille Nonké, *The first man*[1]

This character who lives here, he was the first human being. This individual [*half-man, half-woman*][2] was the tribe's first inhabitant, our ancestors didn't exist. He died, and several years later our elders came and settled here in the tribe.

This individual who once lived here is called Bwîhîcîî. Nobody would walk by down there. He'd catch people and eat them raw. He would choose someone rather portly, he would pinch them to see if there was much to eat on them before killing them to eat them raw.

His skeleton was in this cave, but it has disappeared. Destroyed by the years, we're not sure where it is anymore.

It's the end of the story. It's finished.

---

* Dr Claire Moyse-Faurie collected, transcribed, and translated this oral history into French and graciously gave permission for it to be published in this English translation for the first time.
† Claire Moyse-Faurie is Professor Emeritus at the French National Centre for Scientific Research (CNRS). She holds a PhD in linguistics from Université Paris 5 and lives in Paris, France.
‡ Daryl Morini is editor of *Synkrētic*. He holds a PhD in International Relations (UQ) and is based in Canberra.

II
Philibert Nékaré, *On Kanak men and women*[3]

I would like to speak to you about the way of life of the Kanak [*Indigenous New Caledonian*] man. Kanak men see themselves as pine trees while the others, women…women, we Xârâgurè people compare Kanak woman to a poplar tree, and man to a pine tree.

The pine tree, that's the chief of the family, the tribe, and the clan.

And women have many meanings, which people have forgotten. Woman is the poplar. It is she who gives life, who multiplies the clans, who makes the clan multiply, woman does.

This is what the elders say, that it's the beginning and the end, the magnania plant, the beginning and the end, woman is. She makes clans multiply by their roots. We are here through her. We meet each other thanks to women.

The elders say we come from one single belly. We eat one single share of food, we make sacred one single clan thanks to one woman, this woman who multiplies the clan. That's it.

This is how we speak. White people express themselves in their own way but it all comes to the same, when speaking of women white people say the same thing.

Woman is the Kanak poplar, she multiplies the clan. He, the pine tree, the male, stays upright, he stays upright, he is the chief. He is upright in the clan, in the family, in the council of chiefs.

That's custom, that's how we see ourselves in our Xârâgurè land.

III
Marinette Oundo, *The women of Koum*[4]

Koum is up there in the mountain range, a mountain peak where the elders once lived in the time of the elders.

Thus, in the time of the elders the people in that part of the mountain range never went fishing. They never went fishing. They'd wait for the coastal people to come up to meet them to trade their products, exchanging seafood for goods from the land. They'd come from above, they'd come down and meet up. They'd come down with goods from the land. They'd meet people from the coast who would come up to give their seafood. They'd meet them and they'd give them their seafood, then they would ascend from there, where they'd met, while the others went back down.

One day, three women decided to defy this taboo that the elders had decreed. They wanted to see the seashore. They know that they will have to hide at night. They go fishing down by the sea, they want to go see what it's like on the seashore. They will set off while the others are still asleep. They will go down to the seashore. They'll come down and find that spot where they know they'll be able to fish, to quickly fish during the night, and they'll head back up while the elders are still asleep.

These women went down. They went all the way to the seashore and began to fish. They fish and fish. They pick up shells and fill baskets with them. When their baskets are full, they figure that they should start to head back up.

One goes ahead and starts to climb the mountain as she sees that dawn is upon them, that dawn is coming from over there. She tells the other two to hurry up and climb. She starts to climb the mountain but thus it is that the sun is rising, and she is turned to stone on the way up, while another is changed to stone on the seashore, and the third was changed to stone on the reef.

It's all over, the sun caught them by surprise. They transgressed the words that the elders had spoken, those which exist and that we explain in the tribe. This is how we do it: we meet, we trade, and it's finished. These women, they came from up there, they did this, they went fishing.

That's it, they went back up, the sun rose, it was over. So, the elders saw it and it's as if they had put a curse on them. They cursed them because they had transgressed.

One climbed up the mountain, she will stay there for all time on the mountain side. One sits here, the other there. Nowadays, these women sit there today. They never came back to the Koum tribe.

That's how it is, they transgressed the tabou, the proscribed behaviours. That which the elders had put in place. They remain sitting for all time, they have turned to stone, these women are here until this day. They turned to stone, these women, and are seated there today, even to this day they're still seated in those stony areas up there today, these women. It's those stones we can see today. They are seated over there to this day.

That's why when the elders talk about certain behaviours to abide by, you have to really listen, because if you don't listen to what you have to do, something might well happen to you.

Well, that's what happened to those women. They sit there forever. That's why when you pass by on your boat, we say that it's the Koum women sitting there. They're sitting over there. The story is over.

IV

Marceline Até, *The sacred eel*[5]

So, there is a little creek, its name is Fabwèèwi, in my father's field. There is a lizard there. Okay, I will tell its story. There was a day, some time ago, when my dad went, he went to clear his coffee plantation. It's far off in the distance. He arrives on his coffee plantation, he starts to clear the field as he enters it.

An elder comes by. That elder is a mountain. A mountain that looks like an island. It's sloped, with trees growing on it. And there are stones on its back. Lots of different weeds grow on it.

The mountain gradually comes down. It comes down, and down, and down, it finds the old man by the little creek, where he is clearing his coffee plantation.

A cry rings out, getting louder and louder. It's the mountain. It's singing, crowing like a rooster.

The old man searches around, he looks and sees an eye that's moving. He speaks to it: 'Hey, you there! Keep going! I didn't come here to bar your path. I came to clear my coffee plantation.'

The mountain has by now come down and drops where the two creeks branch off. It was shaped like an island. It stayed there for all time. This island has always stayed there. Now, we're beginning to do things on it.

It is divided into two small creeks. One of those creek forks is good. But the other one, we used to go fishing in it before, only catching bits of eel…its head, tail, and body. All the bits would wriggle. This is a sacred place. The elders have said that it's now fine for us to use. But we aren't allowed to go and eat the bits of eel. Or else we'll fall sick.

But the name of that creek is Fabwèèwi. Fabwèèwi, well, on one side it's good but bad on the other. Famûnaawè is one of the creek's forks, the other side is Fabwèèwi.

It's finished.

V

Maria Thavivianon, *The chief's chicken*[6]

There once lived a chief, the chief of the Ema tribe. He used to feed a chicken. There was another person, this person killed and stole the chicken, cooking it to eat it.

The chief awaits the chicken, calls the chicken, the chicken isn't there. He thinks that maybe he, the other man, had killed it. He calls it.

The man is questioned, he questions him. The man says that he's not the one who killed the chicken.

The chief calls everyone. They discuss the theft, and the disappearance of the chief's chicken. They interrogate the suspect who says that, no, he's not the one who killed the chicken.

So, the chief says: 'I will call my chicken.' He calls it. He calls the chicken. The chicken responds, it responds from inside the man's stomach. 'Well, you said you weren't the one who killed the chicken, and yet the chicken has made its first cluck! It squawked in your stomach, you've already eaten it.'

The chief punished him with labour for having lied as well as for the theft.

That's the end.

Notes

1 Corneille Nonké, 'Le premier homme', October 2010, in Claire Moyse-Faurie, *Field archives from New Caledonia*, Pangloss Collection, CNRS, available at: <https://pangloss.cnrs.fr/corpus/show?lang=fr&mode=normal&oai_primary=cocoon-527ca321-1ed8-3477-b19b-78c5056e8340>.

2 Notes in square brackets are provided in the researcher's original French transcript.

3 Philibert Nékaré, 'Kamûrû ngürü the Kanak', 12 October 2010, Pangloss Collection, CNRS, available at: <https://pangloss.cnrs.fr/corpus/show?oai_primary=cocoon-ca3f4452-c1ed-4c89-9b78-b88eda4d1dec >.

4 Marinette Oundo née Tonwiri sii., 'Story about women of Koum', 14 October 2010, Pangloss Collection, CNRS, available at: <https://pangloss.cnrs.fr/corpus/show?oai_primary=cocoon-da586a73-2cd9-41a4-b13b-7a0b264fd19f>.

5 Marceline Até, 'Anguille sacrée', 6 November 2010, Pangloss Collection, CNRS, available at: <https://pangloss.cnrs.fr/corpus/show?oai_primary=cocoon-1a8d9eec-88db-47dc-a55c-410ec56285fe>.

6 Maria Thavivianon, 'Histoire du coq d'Ema', 7 November 2010, in Claire Moyse-Faurie, *Field archives from New Caledonia*, Pangloss Collection, CNRS, available at: <https://pangloss.cnrs.fr/corpus/show?oai_primary=cocoon-72d15667-9e75-3953-9a93-e1c29fd04d46>.

NOTES

REVIEW

Daya Krishna and Twentieth-Century Indian Philosophy by Daniel Raveh

*Ben Gaskin**

> "'I understand a text better,' DK says, 'when I ask myself what this person [the author] is trying to do. I make that text my own...I get into this work, into his thought process...and carry it in a direction where it was not taken.'"[1]

We might here open with a quote from Daya Krishna himself, that is DK as Raveh refers to him and as we shall also here. The text in question, that which we are trying to understand, is Daniel Raveh's *Daya Krishna and Twentieth-Century Indian Philosophy*, published in 2020. The difficulty with this particular text—or rather, with taking DK's advice seriously in our efforts—is that our task is here twofold.

The first layer is simple, we want to understand what Raveh has done. The second, meanwhile, requires us also to keep in mind that DK himself is an active participant in this ongoing conversation. This becomes further complicated when we enter the room that Raveh has set up to find a whole cast of characters, some perhaps familiar, others unknown. The layers, therefore, are Raveh, DK, and a whole cast of the most prominent figures in twentieth-century

---

* Ben Gaskin researches Jain and Aristotelian logics. He holds a Master's with first class honours in philosophy from the University of Auckland and lives in Auckland, New Zealand.

Review: *Daya Krishna and Indian Philosophy*

Indian philosophy with whom DK was himself in dialogue throughout his life, which conversation forms the central thread of Raveh's text.

The structure of this book reflects the multiplicity of interests which absorbed DK during his life, both philosophical and political. This can be seen already in the layout that Raveh has selected. Chapter one is titled 'Toward a New Picture of Indian Philosophy' and broadly summarises DK's involvement in Indian philosophy, particularly his efforts to integrate and stimulate the further development of this field. Chapter two, 'Thinking Creatively about the Creative Act,' approaches most plainly the condition of a conversation. Raveh interposes his own commentary with excerpts from DK's own article. The resulting chapter is a true dialogue between the two writers. The third chapter, 'Freedoms', concerns DK's notion of freedom—that it is, as evident from the plural, not a singular term nor can be understood as such. And the fourth and final chapter, 'Concepts and Actions,' deals mainly with the way in which DK's writing and involvement extended beyond the strictly academic to include social and political concerns.

While we might proceed plainly to deal with each chapter in turn, this would hardly reflect the approach endorsed by DK himself as outlined in the above excerpt. Instead of simply repeating what Raveh is saying in his text, therefore, we will rather seek ourselves to enter into this ongoing conversation, one which has continued all the while within Raveh despite DK's passing away in 2007. We will, in doing so, make the same disclaimer as that which Raveh makes concerning his interpretation of DK. This disclaimer reflects a basic principle of DK's philosophy, namely that he ardently opposed pretensions to univocality. This might seem to emerge as much from DK's political notions of the proper place of philosophy, and more broadly of thought in society, as it does also from his sensitive treatment and centering of the philosophy of language. Thus, his careful policy is here at once descriptive and prescriptive, that we neither can nor ought to seek to define exclusively. If this seems to contradict the role of a reviewer, then so be it.

Synkrētic

Indeed, here we have touched most directly upon what seems the central thread running through both DK's corpus and Raveh's text. This can be understood by returning to the metaphor with which we began, that of a conversation. Raveh's efforts amount, in effect, to an invitation to a party at which DK was present and spoke throughout the night on a vast variety of topics. Yet we can note that, despite the numerous topics touched upon, across all of these DK demonstrates a consistent personality. It is perhaps here that we might most properly begin: Raveh's text is an introduction to the formidable personality of his friend Daya Krishna.

We can understand our own encounter with DK as proceeding in terms like those discussed in chapter three concerning art and creativity, namely that we are invited into a world in which things are not bound by the necessity of existence. The world in which we find ourselves is instead co-constituted by Raveh and DK, and in this it offers something new.

As DK himself put it: 'Art is an invitation from one person to another to enter into a world where necessity is minimised and freedom is maximised.'[2] Here we may not immediately understand philosophy as an artistic endeavour, yet DK insists on the similarity of the creative act across modalities. The effect of the enterprise, whether artistic or philosophical, is likewise similar. As Raveh says of DK, 'These visits to other realms, freer realms, are significant, he believes, if and only if they transform and enrich the world one returns to.'[3]

We see here that our encounter with DK in the world of thought which he has woven for us is intended to be meaningful in the sense Heidegger spoke of: 'If the answer could be given, the answer would consist in a transformation of thinking, not in a propositional statement about a matter at stake.'[4] This effect, clearly interwoven throughout the entirety of DK's corpus, emerges as his essential aim.

The world into which we are invited, however, is not static but dynamic. It is a living whole. DK holds firmly that the ideal for philosophical work is not a textbook of answers, but is merely to offer, as Raveh puts it, 'a window through which the reader can look into the author's creative thinking process.'[5] This ongoing process is not one in which the viewer is merely a passive observer. It requires their active participation in thinking through the thoughts which are first presented only as dead symbols on a page. The text is incomplete absent the active participation of its recipient, and this not as audience but also as interlocutor. Here we may recall the quote from DK featured at the outset, in which he outlines his ideal for this active participation. As he says elsewhere, 'one cannot understand any work unless one ceases to see it as a finished product.'[6] The ideal for philosophical and artistic endeavours more broadly, therefore, is that one should see each piece as merely reflecting a 'temporary halting place' in the broader dance of thought and creative activity.[7] This is a dance as old as time. As Raveh describes it, 'DK is interested in the collective, perennial process that they [*i.e.* each individual work] are an instant of.'[8]

DK emphasises this process view of philosophical practice in his treatment of Indian philosophy in particular. For instance, he speaks of the Samvad Project—his effort along with several colleagues to open up a dialogue between two streams within the living process of Indian philosophy—as 'something like the Sangam at Prayag Raj.'[9] Raveh explains that this refers to 'the famous confluence of Ganga and Yamuna [rivers] near Allahabad.'[10] The two movements brought together here, Ganga and Yamuna, are the classical tradition of Indian philosophy as practiced in Sanskrit and the more modern mode of Indian philosophy as practiced primarily in English. DK's aim in this seems to have been for its practitioners to become more self-conscious of the breadth and depth of Indian philosophy.

Here the historical context is important, in that the intrusion of British colonisation created a bifurcation of the rivers of Indian thought, creating well-funded colonial universities and yet leaving intact, albeit neglected, traditional centres of Indian thought. DK sought to merge these streams and to take a step towards reforming the self-conscious unity of Indian philosophy. The two streams were brought together in a series of dialogues 'between active practitioners of the two philosophical traditions, the Indian and the

Synkrētic

Western, in a dialogical situation where each was forced to existentially face the living tradition of a different way of philosophizing.'[11]

The aim of the Samvad Project can be summarised by a phrase reflecting a thread that runs throughout DK's corpus: 'when people gather together, something new emerges.'[12] This emphasis on multivocality is coupled in DK with a steadfast faith in the possibility of newness. His method was movement in thought wherever possible, particularly in relation to the state of Indian philosophy. In an excerpt with which many younger scholars may empathise, he says that

> a picture once built is difficult to dismantle, but the evidence and the argument slowly undermine it, and the younger generation which is not so indissolubly "wedded" to "orthodoxy" as the older one, begins to be more open and responsive to the critique as it finds some substance in it.[13]

Here, in an excerpt from the introduction to his *New Perspectives*, DK takes aim at the prevailing concept of Indian philosophy. One of DK's key targets in this endeavour was the contrast between Western civilisation as 'rational' and Indian civilisation as 'spiritual.' This notion, he emphasised, did not merely take the form of an external stereotype: 'What the British produced was a strange species... [whose] terms of reference are the West.'[14]

We may note that here DK's thought entails a distinctively political aspect, which may be seen throughout his corpus. This tendency towards politicised, minority views earned for DK the reputation of a maverick philosopher. Raveh reports that a professor at an esteemed Indian university remarked to him that 'Daya Krishna was a great man... but very provocative.'[15] This view can be seen as a natural consequence of DK's self-appointed task, which Raveh elsewhere describes as 'to shoot question-arrows at "the beliefs," many of them "totally unfounded," that constitute the conventional picture of Indian philosophy.'[16] This habit extended to his reading of the canonical texts, which others tended to treat as beyond reproach. G.R. Malkani, for instance, pointedly questioned whether DK was 'competent to find fault with the father of the system'—that is, with Sankara, generally regarded as the founder of the Vedānta school of Indian philosophy. The significance of DK's approach, Raveh notes, is that he did not see Sankara as a father 'but as a fellow-thinker, an interlocutor, even if more than a thousand years separated them.'[17] As Raveh further remarks:

> DK is well aware that this textual approach is hardly accepted by the traditionalist, who prefers that the texts that he holds precious remain 'untouched' by a sharp philosophical scalpel such as DK's.[18]

This sense of DK's apparent disrespect was likely only increased by the fact that he seemed to be playing a different game entirely. He did not seek to substitute his own views. We might instead compare his approach to that of Nietzsche, in that he likewise sought to philosophise with a hammer:

> This little book is a *grand declaration of war*, and as regards the sounding-out of idols, this time they are not idols of the age but *eternal* idols which are here touched with the hammer as with a tuning fork—there are no more ancient idols in existence ... Also none more hollow... That does not prevent their being the *most believed in*; and they are not, especially in the most eminent case, called idols ...[19]

Where such idols are found empty, where they ring hollow, then DK is not reticent to take the hammer to them. This is not intended merely as a destructive act, but rather that he might thereby clear the ground for new growth. We might imagine this metaphorically by reflecting upon the dynamics of a forest in which ancient trees stand tall above the undergrowth below, blocking the sunlight whereby these saplings might have had a chance to reach their full potential. DK here plays the part of a careful woodsman, inspecting old trees for weakness and rot, then, where necessary, striking to make way for something new.

Of course, this metaphor is itself overly destructive and misrepresents DK's true stance towards India's extant traditions. This is readily apparent in his view that

> Philosophical schools do not die of criticism. Rather, they get a new life and rigour as they try to meet the challenge, usually introducing interesting modifications in their position, or different arguments in support of their

position. The history of philosophy, in all traditions, is the history of counter-argument.[20]

The idea is not, therefore, that these should be destroyed outright; it is not tradition with which DK was at war. He was opposed only to the univocality of a presumptuous and suffocating authority. This was the target of his ire, not Indian traditions as such but only in this negative aspect. Here DK must not be seen as merely tearing down false idols. The purpose of this enterprise was to give new life to Indian philosophy, that he might thus be an exemplar of one who could seek newness even in the most ancient of traditions. We see in this side of DK a maverick philosopher, no doubt, but one whose mission was to encourage the participation of new voices in a hitherto hidebound discourse. This is why he was not interested in using his talents to institute a new regime. It was always the questions in which he was interested. Answers close a door; they pretend that the process is complete. Questions are an open door and every answer—if taken honestly and without pretension—itself brings into being a whole raft of new questions. The movement of philosophy, for DK, is a never-ending story.

For those operating outside of India, whether in the Western tradition or otherwise, this message must be seen as equally applicable to our own experience. This is particularly pertinent because, as DK recognised, social and technological developments are reshaping the world of thought. While the importance of tradition remains, the present conditions demand an imaginative effort to think through the relation between thought and the ever-changing actuality to which it refers. DK thus speaks of, in Raveh's words, 'the need of philosophy to calibrate itself to the present, lest it become a prehistoric dinosaur.'[21] We can sense in DK's corpus a sense of urgency, that he truly believes in the importance of philosophy to the world. Yet it is clear that he believes that this significance is not merely a *de facto* state but rather must be achieved by the efforts of its practitioners. If philosophy merely claims for itself this title *a priori*, then it will only drift further and further from true relevance for its never knowing that it needed to move. This is only one aspect of the importance of DK's work to the modern world more broadly. While the title's reference to the twentieth century and Indian philosophy may lead some to believe that it is a work limited to both particulars, the nature of DK's mission is plainly of universal relevance today.

Of course, this is not to minimise the essentially Indian focus of DK's work and Raveh's text alike. Throughout the book we are introduced to a whole swathe of characters, most of whom are known only within India. These characters, thanks to Raveh's detailed introductions to aspects of their thought, may provide a jumping-off point for further inquiries into Indian philosophy. This is a text which admirably embodies the principle DK himself set out, that 'when people gather together, something new emerges.'[22] This book offers us an introduction to a range of impressive thinkers, both in the classical and modern Indian traditions, with whose works we may go on to pursue a dialogue at our leisure. We can thus read Raveh's work as opening up a conversation between ourselves as readers and DK, as well as a variety of other thinkers, Indian and Western alike. This is not a text, in other words, from which one ought to seek certain answers. It is rather a party whose host introduces us to a variety of guests. The aim is that we may find new friends as well as—with Daya Krishna's insistent encouragement—our own voice.

Notes

1 Daya Krishna in Daniel Raveh, *Daya Krishna and Twentieth-Century Indian Philosophy* (London: Bloomsbury Academic, 2020), 77.
2 Krishna in Raveh, *Daya Krishna*, 97.
3 Krishna in Raveh, *Daya Krishna*, 97.
4 Martin Heidegger, *On Time and Being*, transl. Joan Stambaugh (Chicago: University of Chicago Press, 2002), 55.
5 Raveh, *Daya Krishna*, 1.
6 Krishna in Raveh, *Daya Krishna*, 86.
7 Krishna in Raveh, *Daya Krishna*, 86.

Synkrētic

8   Raveh, *Daya Krishna*, 86.
9   Krishna in Raveh, *Daya Krishna*, 4.
10 Raveh, *Daya Krishna*, 4.
11 Krishna in Raveh, *Daya Krishna*, 3.
12 Krishna in Raveh, *Daya Krishna*, 37.
13 Krishna in Raveh, *Daya Krishna*, 11.
14 Krishna in Raveh, *Daya Krishna*, 11.
15 Raveh, *Daya Krishna*, 22.
16 Raveh, *Daya Krishna*, 9.
17 Raveh, *Daya Krishna*, 64.
18 Raveh, *Daya Krishna*, 10.
19 Friedrich Nietzsche, *Twilight of the Idols and the Anti-Christ*, transl. R.J. Hollingdale (London: Penguin, 1990), 3.
20 Krishna in Raveh, *Daya Krishna*, 57-58.
21 Raveh, *Daya Krishna*, 7.
22 Krishna in Raveh, *Daya Krishna*, 134.

Synkrētic
SUBMISSIONS

Australia and its place in the world continue to evolve. Now more than ever, we have to understand our region and our place in it. *Synkrētic* is an outlet for thought-provoking writing on philosophy, literature and cultures, from and about the Indo-Pacific. It aims to showcase the diverse traditions of thought, story-telling and expression which are woven into the living tapestry of this culturally, linguistically and politically complex region. We're looking above all for well-written and substantive pieces for publication in the following formats.

Essays	3000 - 6000 words
Stories	≤ 8000 words
Responses	800 - 1600 words
Translations	≤ 8000 words
Notes	300 - 3000 words

For details and guidelines:
synkretic.com

www.ingramcontent.com/pod-product-compliance
Lightning Source LLC
Chambersburg PA
CBHW020327010526
44107CB00054B/2010